More Praise for
Hope for a Better World!

AN ORIGINAL THINKER who is passionately hopeful for humanity, Walters examines why intentional communities so often fail, even when sincere, enthusiastic people set out with determination to build community. But well-meaning desire isn't the only prerequisite to successful creation or fostering of community, and many wannabe communities fail dismally, discouraging future attempts or engendering cynicism. Walters reveals hidden legacies from philosophers of the past that influence our thinking today—how their conceptions of the individual in relation to society directly affect our current relationships. He is really onto something when he calls us heirs, for good or ill, of Malthus, Machiavelli, Adam Smith, Karl Marx, and more. Walters' intention is to clear out deadwood, but also to supply us with fresh building material. With shifts in thinking that are not that difficult, more and more successful communities could blossom. This book cries out for further study and commentary.

—NAPRA ReView

Walters brings us new hope by pointing to human potentials deeper than materialistic and Darwinian expectations. This is not a "utopian" work. Its reasoned analyses are based on clear and demonstrated facts.

—Maria Donzelli, Professor of the History of Philosophy,
Oriental Institute of Naples, Italy

Walters reviews the thinking, conclusions, and errors of many of the great, significant minds of past centuries and culls from that rich body of information insights for a better world, seeded in the cooperative community.

—David Feinstein, Ph.D., co-author The Mythic Path

HOPE FOR A BETTER WORLD!

THE SMALL COMMUNITIES SOLUTION

J. DONALD WALTERS

ISBN: 1-56589-170-8
Printed in Canada

3   5   7   9 10 11   8   6   4   2

Crystal

Clarity

Crystal Clarity Publishers
14618 Tyler-Foote Road
Nevada City, CA 95959-8599

Phone: 800-424-1055 or 530-478-7600
Fax: 530-478-7610
E-mail: clarity@crystalclarity.com
Website: www.crystalclarity.com

Library of Congress Cataloging-in-Publication Data:

Walters, J. Donald.
  Hope for a better world! : the small communities solution/
J. Donald Walters.
      p. cm.
Includes bibliographical references and index.
  ISBN 1-56589-170-8
  1. Community. 2. Cooperativeness. I. Title.
  HM756 .W36 2002
  307--dc21
                                    2002002382

CONTENTS

FOREWORD

I am amazed by this book. I find here for the first time a thesis, acceptable because supported by practical wisdom, on how to create a better life on earth. For those who dream of seeing true peace on earth someday, *Hope for a Better World!* offers a convincing blueprint. In a progressive series of deeply insightful analyses, J. Donald Walters examines why certain societies of the past failed, and how others in future might succeed. His reflections are the most persuasive I've ever encountered.

In classes that I teach at the University of Hawaii and elsewhere, I have been surprised at how many students nowadays express frustration at the absence of flexibility in their lives. They feel locked into their cultural heritage. In this respect, Honolulu is, itself, a laboratory, for in this city people from many traditions, both Eastern and Western, live together, trying to adapt to, and even evolve, a new society. Those who once came here from many countries felt a need to weave about themselves a sort of mental cocoon. That very cultural isolation now often seems artificial to many of their descendants, who want to spread their wings like the butterfly emerging from its cocoon, and to soar in a new reality. Naturally, they are also somewhat fearful concerning their new directions. This book may offer them the clarity they've been seeking. I now feel that I, too, have practical answers to give them. I recommend *Hope for a Better World!* unreservedly. It shows how to draw the best from every culture, and to unite those "bests" in a new future.

This book is not revolutionary. It doesn't reject past wisdom. It is even-handed, intelligent, and respectful of the genius every culture possesses. At the same time, it repeatedly asks a very simple, indeed obvious, question: "Does it work?" It asks also, How? and, Why?

The author has taken upon himself the awesome task of creating places where his ideas could be tested and refined. Increasing numbers—hundreds, now—reside in those communities. They are developing a pattern of living that is above all, in a human sense, realistic. His book is grounded in more than one discipline: scientific, philosophical, and the humanities. He has resolved a major problem that faces anyone who would build communities: how to enable people to live together happily while at the same time challenging and inspiring them to develop their fullest potentials.

To my mind, this last feature, inspiration, is one thing that makes this book so special. Apart from the clear way it addresses real needs, Walters inspires. He actually infuses this quality into his style of writing. His ability to affect the reader's *consciousness*, and not only to persuade us with clear reasoning, is to my mind an amazing feature of this book.

Among my students, what I've noticed is their increasing sense that business skills need to be balanced with spiritual values. Spirituality, Walters insists, means more than adhering to the religious duties prescribed by various traditions. It means striving toward joyful personal transformation. And it means also sharing one's deeper aspirations with others. Spirituality is not a question of converting anyone to anything. True personal fulfillment requires us to feel concerned for others, and to reject the modern-day emphasis on competition.

These are simple concepts—indeed, they seem self-evident. I've often wondered, since reading this work, why they haven't been proposed with such clarity before. Surely they resonate with the way all of us think during moments of calmness.

The communities Walters has established successfully have been an acid test for his ideas. *Hope for a Better World!* suggests that a shining future indeed awaits mankind. I consider this book to be a *must read* for everyone. It will be especially helpful for those who have been struggling to cope with the aftermath of 9/11. And it will help all who sincerely want to improve the quality of life on this planet.

Milton Staackmann
M.A. Cultural Anthropology (University of Hawaii)
teacher, medical researcher

CHAPTER ONE

✽

The Utopian Dream

There is a natural longing in human nature for an ideal society. We see this longing expressed in the popularity of books through the ages that have depicted societies of peaceful, high-minded citizens living together in friendliness, cooperation, and harmony. The story of the Garden of Eden has ageless appeal. Indeed, the idea of a state where human perfection existed, and where all the people were honest, truthful, innocent, and kind carries almost the suggestion of a racial memory.

In recent centuries, that dream has been pilloried. The exploded myth of Nazism (Hitler's German National Socialist Workers Party); of dictatorial communism and its brutish "dictatorship of the proletariat"; harsh present realities (so different, alas, from lofty first expectations) in the American "dream," and the disappointment new societies face everywhere: In these we see justified the growing cynicism that is evident all around us.

We live in an age of social, moral, ideational, and spiritual confusion. Values are often dismissed as "merely relative" and therefore lacking in objective validity. Our basest instincts are paraded before us as the essence of who we really are, as human beings. Beauty in the arts is belittled, and the ugliest distortions of a fevered imagination are defended in the name of honest self-expression.

The purpose of this book is to help you to thread your way past errors that have to a great extent distracted people's understanding. My aim is not to concentrate deeply on the problems (they are obvious enough!), but wherever possible to look for solutions. I hope, moreover, to offer real solutions, and not merely to nibble away with a few minor objections at the edges of each problem. I'd like, wherever opportunity opens the door, to propose sweeping answers. Ultimately I'll offer a sort of "unified field theory" of human progress. Will I succeed? or am I being merely presumptuous? That is for you to decide. Many of the writers whose ideas I'll critique were men of insight. All of them, certainly, were intelligent. Indeed, they are considered geniuses.

Sometimes, however, the questions people address, especially people of keen intelligence, miss issues that touch our lives most closely as human beings. First, an abstraction is proposed; then it is discussed heatedly for decades or even centuries. And then, to everyone's astonishment, someone comes along and—like the child when he beheld the emperor's new (but imaginary) suit of clothes—cries out, "Why, that's the wrong question! What you've been saying is interesting, no doubt, but it misses the point. It leads nowhere. And it diminishes our understanding, rather than increasing it. Let's be not only intelligent: Let us be practical!"

Sometimes it is helpful to step back from an argument and ask oneself, "What is this *really* all about?" Intelligence, when it sets itself up as the only arbiter, can deceive. Important also in the pursuit of truth is the calm, unanswerable impulse within us which says, "Both sides make sense, but this one *feels* true, whereas that other one doesn't." If it should happen that logic supports both sides, wisdom tells us to abide by what, in inner calmness, feels right. Actually, it is not unusual for both sides to be right, each in its own way. In this case, compromise may produce deeper understanding.

My hope is, by avoiding unrealistic "solutions"—like those proposed in books that champion utopia, for example—to show that a way may indeed be found out of the dark labyrinth of cynicism into a sunny world of promise which, so our hearts tell us, surely awaits mankind someday, somewhere, somehow. Indeed, if the future holds nothing better for us than the past, worn to deep ruts as it was by old habits of thinking, then life itself can hardly fail to end up a wasteland. For, despite anything science can do about it, mankind faces the bleak prospect of cities doomed to increasing congestion, increasing tension and anxiety, increasing water and air pollution, and increasing damage of a subtler kind also: mental, moral, and spiritual. Solutions *must* be found, for mankind is rapidly losing faith in anything except what Ayn Rand praised with childish arrogance as "The great God, Ego."

Toward the end of the eighteenth century, Thomas Malthus published a book on the improbability that man will ever develop an ideal world. Many people of his day dreamed of a future paradise on earth, where prosperity, brotherhood, and happiness would prevail universally. Malthus titled his book, *An Essay on the Principle of Population.* It was only 50,000 words long, yet it attacked with crystal-clear logic the hope for social perfection.

The paper's full title was, *An Essay on the Principle of Population as it Affects the Future Improvement of Society, with Remarks on the Speculations of Mr. Godwin, Mr. Condorcet, and Other Writers.* William Godwin in England and the Marquis de Condorcet in France had, along with others, envisioned a golden future for mankind, a world of utter—though utterly unrealistic—perfection. Their rainbow balloons positively invited pricking, and it was Thomas Malthus, finally, who did the job using the sharp needle of common sense. In so doing, to general dismay, he laid bare harsh facts that deeply disturbed many people. With youthful exuberance, but incontrovertibly (within his own context), he pointed out that human nature causes the population of the world to increase by geometric progression, whereas the earth's capacity to feed its inhabitants can only increase by arithmetic progression. In time, he declared, the first progression is bound to smash head-on against the solid wall of the second, and people everywhere will starve. Only temporary impediments can delay this process: setbacks in the timing caused by such disasters (decidedly unparadise-like!) as war, poverty, disease, and natural cataclysms. In the absence of such miseries, the geometric increase must continue unchecked.

Godwin and Condorcet had invited the ice bath of realism into which Malthus dumped their theories! Indeed, his logic has never so far been conclusively refuted, although science has managed to delay his bleak day of reckoning somewhat.

Other factors, too, have temporarily postponed the disaster owing to another aspect of human nature: man's lust for committing mayhem. Human beings have annihilated their fellows by the millions. The Khmer Rouge decimated the population of Cambodia on the absurd premise that people's class, training, and social status wholly defined them as human beings. The communist regimes in Russia and China together are "credited" with having killed over a hundred million of their "comrades." World Wars I and II did their own bit in the thinning process. And diseases have brought greater holocausts than any horror of man's doing.

The influenza epidemic of 1918 took more human lives than the entire number of people killed in World War I. The Bubonic Plague of the seven-teenth century wiped out a quarter of the popula-tion of Europe. And in our own day AIDS, Ebola, and other deadly enemies of mankind threaten to wipe out millions, thereby delaying further Malthus's day of reckoning.

Contraception has of course helped to curtail population growth. Yet the explosion continues. Indeed, where religion prohibits contraception the fire has spread unchecked.

It is ironic that well-to-do couples, able to sup-port large families, often have fewer children. At present, population in the wealthier nations is either static or diminishing. Even so, elsewhere in the world, as I've said, the explosion continues.

The reason for this increase lies, one suspects, in Malthus's reminder regarding human nature. Poor people have few pleasures besides sex to divert them. Squalor, moreover, imposes an inadequate diet, which draws the energy, and therefore the con-sciousness, downward in the body, toxically irritat-ing the sex nerves. Other explanations have been given for the relatively large progeny of poor fami-lies. It is said that farmers, for example, need chil-dren to supply free labor for their farms. (Adam Smith had a fair amount to say about the "free" nature of such labor!) One wonders, however, whether many of the poor reason it all out so delib-erately. Sociologists, whose fondness for reasoning induces them to project that predilection onto everyone else, are apt to misread the motives of those less educated than they. Poor people usually have neither the education nor the inclination to view their own future so rationally. Most of them accept what comes, including the children born to them, with a resigned sigh and the rationalization, "If God wants us to have 'em, He'll help us to feed 'em." With or without reason, then, they obey the biblical commandment, "Be fruitful and multiply."

Well-to-do couples, on the other hand, are more likely to plan their future with some care. Financial security gives them a variety of options, and they have many things to satisfy them besides the sex drive. Higher education and a more gracious standard of living provide them with a better diet. These factors all combined help to draw their energy and consciousness upward, instead of keeping them centered in lower, animal drives.

Malthus himself—cynically, one suspects—offered what he must have known was an impracticable solution: He suggested that people either delay marriage until their income rises adequately, or else practice "moral restraint"—that is to say, chastity. Realistically, of course, the poorer classes are the ones least likely to practice self-control of any kind. Few among them would be willing to delay marriage in hope of an unlikely future prosperity, or on the other hand to live together in voluntary chastity. Restraint demands a certain mental equilibrium, which usually is impossible for those whose lives lack outer balance also. It is probable that anyone caught in a tailspin of unpaid bills, screaming children, and the daily trudge between a gray life at home and gray, mindless labor in the factory will not be inclined to exercise any self-control at all.

Fortunately perhaps, Nature does seem to be interesting herself in the problem. Apart from plagues, earthquakes, and other natural catastrophes, the male sperm count has recently measured considerably lower than it once did.

Debates on the issues covered in this book have been pursued with an astonishing degree of anger. One marvels. After all, a proposition is either provable or disprovable. Why get excited about it? Yet, the controversies have raged. Usually, in such matters, that side is the more impressive which answers calmly, with supporting reasons based on solid facts. This consideration alone ought to have had a calming influence on the debate, since facts alone were at issue. Human nature being what it is, however, calmness has often been swept aside. The outrage created by these ideas has been emotional, seldom or never bolstered by objective reasoning, and intensely biased. Max Planck, the famous German physicist, wrote in his *Scientific Autobiography,* "A new scientific truth does not triumph by convincing its opponents and making them see the light, but rather because its opponents eventually die, and a new generation grows up that is familiar with it."

Malthus's essay, though it betrays a certain youthful brashness (he was only thirty-two when his essay was first published), presented known facts, not mere opinions. The storm of controversy it created, however, was based only on opinions, not on facts. William Cobbett referred in writing to "Malthus and his nasty and silly disciples." Religious writers expostulated that Malthus, a clergyman, was wholly devoid of faith in God. Such, indeed, has always been the outcry against new proposals in every field. Critics, finding they couldn't respond with reason, decided their only recourse was to shout.

Commentaries on utopia, too—both for and against the ideal—have been more emotional than reasoned. Plato, the earliest exponent of the ideal society that we know of, was at least reasonable in his presentation—indeed, too reasonable!—as he expounded his concept in *The Republic.*

The word, "utopia," derives from a book by Thomas More, who lived during the reign of Henry VIII (and was executed by him). His book was published first in Latin with the title, *Libellus vere aureus nec minus salutaris quam festivus . . . deque nova Insula Utopia* (not unfashionably long for those days, actually!). Appearing in 1516, the book was an instant success. It was published in English in 1551, sixteen years after the author's death, with a title hardly easier on us today than its Latin version: *A fruteful and pleasaunt Worke of the beste State of a publyque Weale, and of the newe yle, called Utopia.* Literally, the word "utopia" means "no place" (from the Greek *ou,* no, and *topos,* place). More's book was a satire on English society of his day, and offered suggestions for how its prevailing ills might be corrected.

Since that time, other serious writers have proposed what each one thought might be the ideal society. Always, the focus was on the mechanics of social structure, not on attitudes that might be inspired in people as individuals. Notable among these works were *New Atlantis* (1627) by Francis Bacon; *Voyage en Icarie* (1840) by Étienne Cabet; *Looking Backward 2000–1887* (1888) by Edward Bellamy, an American; and *Islandia* (1942) by Austin Tappan Wright.

Columbus's discovery of the New World in 1492 gave people hope that perhaps a sort of earthly Eden might be found at last. The popular imagination soared in anticipation of news that somewhere on earth a noble race had been found. Was the dream of earthly perfection, just possibly, one that would be realized? The French artist Gauguin awakened fantasies of an island paradise in Tahiti when he sailed there and began painting the simple islanders: Had he discovered the innocence described so touchingly by Rousseau in his concept of the "noble savage"? Many people dared hope so.

Reality, however, soon stepped in and punctured, one by one, all those gaily colored balloons.

Copernicus, the founder of modern astronomy (he began his university education in 1491, the year before Columbus "sailed the ocean blue") was the first to unseat man from his throne of dignity in God's universal plan. Until the time of Columbus and Copernicus, people thought the earth was flat and fixed firmly at the center of everything. Columbus, after studying ancient maps, claimed that the world is round, and then proceeded to prove his claim by sailing partway around it to America. Copernicus not long afterward showed empirically that the earth is not stationary, but moves through space. The sun, he said, not the earth, is the center of everything that is. Humanity was demoted in importance, and many people—church dignitaries, notably—didn't like it. It offended their sense of the fitness of things to have some mere contemporary tell them that man was not so essential in the great scheme of things as tradition had taught them to believe!

After Copernicus there followed other pioneers in science such as Galileo Galilei and Isaac Newton. Gradually, amid storms of protest and anathemas, science proceeded to reduce people's self-esteem to the point where it seemed that man's place was not really significant at all. Thus, scientific advancement lured thinking minds away from theology and spiritual matters to the more mundane question of *how,* instead of why, things function as they do. Interest shifted from meaning to mechanisms. With passing time, it became almost *de rigeur* for intellectuals to belittle non-materialistic ideals altogether while boasting their own scientific impersonality.

Thus, in contrast to persisting dreams of social perfection, there arose a growing cynicism, produced to a large extent by the discoveries of science. The Age of Reason in the eighteenth century; the materialistic bias of the nineteenth century; the growing skepticism of the twentieth century: All these caused a widespread loss of faith in transcendent realities of any kind.

Satires were written on the notion of human perfectibility. Famous among these were *Candide* by Voltaire, and Samuel Butler's *Erewhon* (which suggests "nowhere," spelled backward). "Utopia" came in time to be equated with its literal meaning: "Nowhere"—an imaginary place. Thus, it came also to suggest any impractical scheme for social perfectibility.

In biology, Darwin's Theory of Evolution offered the antithesis to the biblical story of creation and to the idyllic existence of Adam and Eve in the Garden of Eden.

In political science, Machiavelli, early in the sixteenth century, was already expressing profound cynicism about the human state. In his treatise, *The Prince,* he offered methods to the rulers of nations for bending the people to their will.

In social theory, Karl Marx proposed, later on, a social order in which the manual laborer is the ideal human being. His "dictatorship of the proletariat" was an emotional reaction against the privileged classes, from which Marx felt that he, too, had been unjustly excluded. What his philosophy did, when stripped to its essence, was present social mechanisms as the entire reality of human existence. Unconscious matter was, to him, the fundamental reality. Genius and high aspiration were fragile superstructures quivering on a bedrock of unheeding Nature. Lofty ideals are, according to his philosophy, mere sentimentalism. Man's reality is animalistic, not spiritual. As for religion—well! that, in his words, is merely "the opiate of the people."

Marx's philosophy was a natural successor to Darwin's theory of evolution. Marx felt he'd discovered the principle of *social* evolution.

Not long after Marx, Sigmund Freud entered the fray, emphasizing "unconscious" drives as the explanation for every aspect of human consciousness.

Pandora's box had by this time been flung open wide. Emotional diatribes against concepts people considered unpalatable tried to slam the lid shut, but all they accomplished was—as in the Greek myth of Pandora—to deny humanity its last remaining "gift": Hope. (The meaning of "Pandora" is "all gifts": *pan,* all, and *dora,* gifts.) By emotionally rejecting what reason had brought out into the open, Hope itself was left "alone and palely loitering" (to quote from the poem by John Keats: "Ah what can ail thee, wretched wight, alone and palely loitering?") Hope, belittled and suppressed, grew pale and sickly. What was left, then? nothing but wishful thinking.

What I'd like to do in this book is, briefly, to look at each of those challenges, investigate their reasoning (though not necessarily to proceed from their premises), and then to suggest new, common-sense answers, or alternatives.

Here, for example, is what might be said in answer to Malthus's dire predictions: Do his statistics really spell doom for humanity? Not at all! They might easily be nullified by worldwide prosperity, as has in fact been suggested. We've seen in fact that prosperity results, generally speaking, in people producing fewer progeny. This fact suggests hope, not despair. Through the pages that follow, and fighting off the hypnosis of a priori assumptions, I will ask: Is this challenge really as threatening as it seems? Does it really presage disaster, or inflict upon us a numbing despair? May not those very facts suggest, when viewed in a new light, a future that promises to be noble and beautiful?

Indeed, though utopia may be too much to hope for, isn't there some reasonable hope, at least, for a *better* future, instead of the certainty of utter ruin?

Back to that question of worldwide prosperity: Is it possible that it may be achieved? Yes, certainly it is! More than possible: It is probable!

How then, do you ask? Please, dear friend and reader, read on.

CHAPTER TWO

✽

Copernicus:
Center, Anyone?

Nicolaus Copernicus was born in Poland in 1473. He died seventy years later, in 1543. His life span covered the middle part of the Renaissance, which closed the door on the Middle Ages and ushered in a new outlook on human life, the world, and the universe.

It was Copernicus who first changed people's anthropocentric outlook. He showed that the earth is not fixed firmly at the center of the universe, but moves around the sun. This discovery was a major factor in loosening the hold of church dogmatism on human thought.

Dogmatism is usually, though not always fairly, identified with church theology. Of course, that word was more or less invented by theologians, but what the church did also was bring to a focus a tendency that is prevalent everywhere. Today, dogmatism is "alive and well"—thriving in fact, even among self-styled iconoclasts. For it is a simple reality of human nature. People like to frame their perception of truth, to focus it narrowly for the sake of clarity, and then to ignore everything outside that frame as though it didn't exist. In fairness, one ought to look at dogmatism from a standpoint of one who sees his belief system—his dogmas—endangered. He fears the loss of that carefully framed view, and forgets that the way he framed it was only an artifice anyway. In fact, what he really fears is loss of control. He feels a personal commitment to his view. His mistake, of course, is that he can never *own* the view: He can only enjoy it. Man thinks of himself as creating, when the best he can do is participate.

Alas, the time even for such participation is so short! A person may invest his entire career in a certain perception of reality, only to find, in the twilight years of his life, some young "upstart" challenging it. Perhaps the older man is already in his sixties when a new discovery is made. He may see it as capable of shattering the frame he constructed so carefully. His productive life is nearly over. Has he wasted it? Has he spent it pursuing a will-o'-the-wisp?

Let us say he is a university professor. His professional standing may seem to be at stake. What will happen, if this new discovery causes a complete shift in people's thinking? He would need courage to admit that for all these years he's been mistaken. He might even prefer honorable death in defense of his country to seeing his hard-earned reputation destroyed. Not many could face with equanimity the fact that convictions they'd held their whole professional lives, and declared proudly and confidently to so many students, were fallacious.

The larger the ship, the harder it is for it to turn quickly. This was the secret of little England's victory against the "Invincible" Spanish Armada in 1588: The Spanish ships were large and ungainly. The English ones were small and could be maneuvered easily.

Dogmatism would have existed with or without the church. What the church did, primarily, was empower people's natural resistance to change.

Before the discoveries of Copernicus it seemed obvious to everyone that the earth was the center of creation. One could see for himself that the sun, moon, stars, and planets all revolved around this central aspect of God's creation. Few people gave much thought to such anomalies as the constellations moving up and down against the horizon as the seasons change. It never occurred to them to question why: These things simply happened.

Humanity's knowledge of the earth itself was very slight compared to what we know today. (An old map in Hakluyt's *Voyages,* published in 1589, had only this to say about regions as yet unexplored: "Here be griffins.") During the Middle Ages, people tended to view even their own countrymen virtually as "foreigners" if they lived a few villages away. As for the universe, they had no conception of how vast it is. To them, reality was relatively cozy: heavenly bodies revolving "up there" solely for the benefit of mankind.

The church gave such concepts as these its stamp of approval. The fact that it did so seemed to justify popular opposition to Copernicus, when the protests began. Copernicus during his lifetime saw the demise of medieval society, and the birth I referred to above of a new outlook on reality.

The Renaissance got its start in Florence, Italy, with people's awakened interest in the culture of ancient Greece. The year 1492 saw the discovery of the New World by Christopher Columbus. Minds were stirred by new possibilities. Soon, walls were crumbling everywhere—ramparts that had stood for centuries protecting the venerable city, Official Dogma.

Copernicus was very different in nature from Thomas Malthus, who lived three centuries later. Malthus almost gleefully challenged some of the basic assumptions of his day. Copernicus, by contrast, was reluctant even to publish his findings. Malthus lived at a time when intellectual impudence could be confident of a hearing. He wrote after the French Revolution, after the American War of Independence, after Voltaire and other free thinkers had urged people to think for themselves, after France's solemn announcement of the dawn of a new "Age of Reason." It was a time when many people found it exhilarating to have their—or perhaps I should say, other people's!—preconceptions shaken by new discoveries. Copernicus, on the other hand, was born at a time when orthodoxy held universal sway. The church, like a large ocean liner, was not able to respond to any sudden call for a change of direction.

It wasn't from the Bible, however, that Rome derived its view of the universe. It accepted this view on scientific authority. Well, such was Rome's way. It asked, "What does authority say?" not, "What do the facts indicate?" Creative thought is anathema to the need of institutions for conformity.

In this case, authority rested in the calculations of Ptolemy, an ancient astronomer of Alexandria. Ptolemy was not a Christian, but his declaration in 150 A.D. (or thereabout) that the universe revolves around the earth was acceptable to the church fathers. It was compatible with what those authorities understood of the Bible, and had, therefore, to be true. What the church in those days declared as true, even in mundane matters, was tantamount to dogma.

When Copernicus realized from his reckoning that Ptolemy had been in error, he feared persecution by the church. According to prevailing opinion, as Robert B. Downs put it in *Books That Changed the World,** "The whole universe seemed to be made for man." The universe had been created by an anthropomorphic Lord, an emperor-God whose

*Revised paperback edition, New American Library, New York (1983).

primary concern was for His human subjects, made, as the Bible tells us, in His own image.

Ptolemy's cosmology was supported not only by the sanction of tradition, but also, so it seemed, by common sense. Copernicus contradicted what everyone could see clearly was a fact. After years of painstaking study of the heavens, he concluded that the earth is not stationary, as everyone believed, but rotates on its axis once a day, and travels around the sun once every year. As Robert Downs expressed it, "So fantastic was such a concept in the sixteenth century that Copernicus did not dare to advance it until he was convinced his data were irrefutable." Even so, it took him thirty years to make his revolutionary "theory" publicly available. No doubt he was deterred partly by fear of the church. Even after that long wait, his findings when announced attracted violent opposition.

Downs tells us, "According to one tale, the printer's shop where *De Revolutionibus* [Copernicus's opus] was being printed was attacked by university students who tried to destroy the press and the manuscript; the printers barricaded themselves to finish the job." The church reacted with resolute opposition to the new theory, especially after its later refinement by Johannes Kepler and Tycho Brahe.

Galileo supported those findings both mathematically and by observation through a telescope, which hadn't been invented while Copernicus was alive. Galileo was fortunate enough to have friends high in the Catholic hierarchy. Nevertheless, even he was forced at last to repudiate his discoveries. Today it seems hardly credible, but Galileo remained guilty of "heresy" in the eyes of the church until late in the twentieth century. Only then, after more than three centuries had passed, was he given official church pardon!

It should be reiterated, however, that it is unfair to blame the church entirely, absurd as it now seems for it to have refused for so long to admit its mistake. For the church recognized that much more was at stake than this simple issue of heliocentricity versus geocentricity. Modern science has shown itself increasingly indifferent to certain attitudes that, in religion, are essential. For example, it has always been condescending toward devotional feeling. Indeed, it considers feeling of any kind detrimental to impersonal objectivity, valued in science above all other attitudes. Devotional attitudes are vitally important in religion. Without them, religion itself might sink to the level of hypocritical mummery. The church felt, understandably, that it had to protect values that to it were so supremely important.

Individually, many scientists have in fact believed in God. Einstein, one of the greatest of them, described scientific discovery in terms of "mystical awe." His transcendent outlook, however, had nothing to do with church affiliation of any kind. Indeed, he was suspicious of any attempt by so-called "authority" to limit the freedom of scientific inquiry.

Long, however, after religion had lost its power to impose concepts or to ban new findings as heretical, dogmatism was still healthy and robust. Other writers, including scientists themselves, adamantly opposed findings that didn't fit into their own carefully constructed beliefs.

The story of Immanuel Velikovsky, in the twentieth century, is a sad example of scholarly persecution. Whether or not his theories were valid, Velikovsky's revolutionary book, *Earth in Upheaval,* about an interplanetary event that, he claimed, had dramatically affected the earth, was at least carefully researched. Yet it was so fiercely excoriated by the scientific "establishment" that many publishers wouldn't even accept more of his writings for publication. Scientists—not bishops and clergymen, mind you, but supposedly impersonal and objective astronomers and physicists— had threatened to boycott those firms.

I was intrigued by another example of emotional outrage by a well-known scientist. In this case, the denunciation was directed at a revolutionary, but well-researched and indeed fascinating book: *The Hidden History of the Human Race,* by Michael A. Cremo and Richard L. Thompson. This book presents startling evidence that *Homo sapiens* may have existed on this planet far longer than is officially accepted. The book won substantial support from authorities in the field, but it was slated by no less a man than Richard Leakey, the internationally known anthropologist. "Your book," wrote Leakey, "is pure humbug and does not deserve to be taken seriously by anyone but a fool." Leakey didn't go so far as to urge persecution of the authors, but his opinion has certainly weighed heavily in anthropological circles. He was influenced in his outburst by convictions that, while by no means founded in religious dogma, were nevertheless, in their own way, dogmatically religious. The displeasure he evinced was with ideas that threatened to undermine his own carefully structured understanding of human evolution.

To reiterate, orthodoxy and dogmatism are not monopolies of the church; they are a common human phenomenon. Clear reason cannot always ensure acceptance for a new truth. People everywhere are inclined to be swayed by "authority," whether it be religious or any other kind.

Gradually, over the centuries since Copernicus discovered that our earth is not the hub of the universe, astronomers have come to realize how very far it is from being the center of anything—except, perhaps, of our own little moon's orbit. (I say "perhaps" because that orbit is elliptical; the earth cannot be exactly at its center.)

Late in the nineteenth century, astronomers found that the sun, too, is not central in the universe, as they'd believed. In time, others discovered that the sun lies near the edge of a vast star system—a galaxy, as it came to be known after the astronomer Hubble, in 1925, discovered that what had been thought was a nebula in Andromeda is in fact another star system like our own. The "Milky Way," as our galaxy has come to be known, was first thought to be only one among several others. Now it is known that at least a hundred billion galaxies exist. In our own Milky Way there are estimated to be over a hundred billion stars. Every galaxy, similarly, is thickly populated with stars.

It was several decades into the twentieth century that the center of the Milky Way was located. It is 27,000 light years away from us. Even the nearest star to the sun is at a distance of four light years. When we consider that light travels at 300,000 kilometers (186,000 miles) *a second,* the mind simply gives up trying to grasp the immensity of it all.

To speak of any point in the universe as the cosmic center would be, itself, pointless. It may be that a center exists, but if it should be found there are few who would consider the fact very significant. Since Copernicus, astronomy has so radically reduced man's consciousness of significance in the great scheme of things that one may wonder if humanity is even relevant to anything.

And yet . . . and yet . . . :

Where we ourselves are concerned, are not we, at least, central to everything we can perceive?

What choice have we, except to begin from this perspective? Although the thought may strike one as medieval with a vengeance, it is quite the opposite, really. For it posits an understanding of everything in existence from an infinity of centers, beginning always from the unique perspective of each one of them. From the concept of a universe without any imaginable center, it is necessary now to contemplate it completely anew: not as a totality that would be comprehensible only from outside—and therefore, as far as man is concerned, not really comprehensible at all—but *from within an infinite number of centers.*

This is how living things grow. They develop outward from their first tiny cell. Their reality is not *formed:* it manifests itself, from that center.

In past ages, hierarchies of aristocrats, usually ruled by a king, were at the apex of a descending order of populace down to the lowest serfs. When kings made war, what they wanted, usually, was to expand their dominion, and of course thereby to increase their own importance. How petty, that ambition! Worldly conquest is always temporary, because artificial. It is an outer imposition on human beings, whose true reality is unassailably locked within themselves. Conquest is possible only, in the truest sense, when it succeeds in winning a voluntary and cooperative response: willingness on the part of others to participate in whatever outward events are occurring.

In terms of the universe, if it is true that the reality of all things begins at their center, then the center of all things must be considered to be everywhere. What no militant ruler can ever accomplish may be achieved easily, not only (as I suggested above) by winning others' consent, but more subtly by consciousness! In sympathy, man's awareness can reach out and embrace everyone and everything. It can touch individual centers everywhere in recognition of their kinship with one's self. Thus, one can not only draw things and people sympathetically to himself: One can understand them deeply, as kindred realities to his own.

Physicists say the atom is the key to the universe. If this is so, it is quite reasonable to consider every atom as, itself, the center of the universe. "Center everywhere, circumference nowhere" was an ancient concept. Only in relation to one atom can everything else be understood. Reality reaches out from its center everywhere toward its own center, everywhere.

How different, this view, from the popular concept of reality!

From people's perception of the earth as fixed and central in creation to the staggering concept that there may be no center anywhere, it is really only a short leap to considering every atom in space, and every "ego-atom" (thus to describe humanity), as a valid point of departure in any search for universal understanding.

This point will become increasingly important in this book. For *no one can understand anything except from **his own** central reality, and from his individual ability to understand.* Even Einstein, universal as his outlook was, could only begin with his own capacity for understanding. The most amazing insights in science are limited by the comprehension of their discoverers.

It will become evident, as we proceed, that only the individual, not society as a whole, can provide a key to social progress as well. Social development begins with one person; it cannot be imposed on society from above, nor from outside. Efforts to improve the human lot by outward means only must fail unless individuals cooperate of their own free will with those efforts. Without their willing cooperation, the most zealous efforts at reformation will inevitably leave humanity more or less where it has always been.

It is easier, certainly, to ponder abstract schemes for perfecting society. It is much more difficult to inspire individuals to embrace change voluntarily. Nevertheless, this is the only method that has a chance of working. If true change is to be effected in this world, it must be inspired in individuals who have a sincere desire for it, themselves.

CHAPTER THREE

❈

Machiavelli and Social Governance

The individual, as we saw at the end of the last chapter, is the key to humanity, even as the atom is the key to the material universe. In anatomy class, medical students are given one cadaver to dissect, not a thousand of them, to help them understand the way the body works. With human nature, similarly, it is enough to know one person deeply. Every human being contains within himself the essence of all humanity, with its potential for ignorance and wisdom, hatred and love, misery and happiness, self-deception and clarity. The counsel of ages has always been: "Know thyself." Who, indeed, can ever know us as deeply as we can know ourselves?

In the past, people saw no need to probe beneath appearances. The study of anatomy wasn't even included in medical training until relatively recently. Doctors prior to 1628 and the publication of William Harvey's *Essay on the Motion of the Heart and the Blood* had no clear understanding of the way blood circulates in the body. Artists prior to Michelangelo had only a dim notion of the inner structure of the body. They depicted people as though the skin covered only smooth flesh. Man's understanding of the universe, equally, was based on casual observation. Sun, moon, and the other heavenly bodies appeared to revolve around the earth; therefore, that was what they did. The earth looked flat: therefore, it *was* so. (One wonders what the mariner made of ships, approaching from a distance, as they rose out of a seemingly flat sea!) As things appeared to be, so by common agreement they were.

There were great works of literature, certainly, and great paintings and sculptures, that evidenced deep insight into human nature. Those exceptions, however, only proved the rule: It was self-knowledge that gave their creators a clear perception of the subtleties of the human mind.

Social philosophy, too, was focused on society as a whole, not on individuals. Treatises dealt with the classes of society, while paying slight heed to human beings. Governance was understood as a means of controlling the populace, not of benefiting them or of alleviating their miseries.

A society, however, is made up of individuals. They are not mere statistics: They are flesh and blood. People cannot be understood merely from their social status. Rather, society can be rightly understood only in terms of its citizens, and of their particular needs and interests.

Important as the individual is, however, it must

always be kept in mind that systems are important, too. What is being proposed in this book, then, is not some newly disguised form of anarchy, but only a shift in emphasis—away from people *en masse* to people as individuals.

The universe itself is systematic, not random. Planets move in regular orbit around their stars; stars revolve around their galactic centers. In public affairs, similarly, some sort of system is necessary. (Imagine the modern freeway as a free-for-all!) People are thinking beings, and cannot but have differences of opinion on countless subjects. They may express their differences amicably, or do so with heated passion. They may relinquish their own opinions for the sake of over-all harmony. But to expect everyone to agree, or to resolve differences voluntarily, would be unrealistic. Every group needs a leader; someone to inspire it, to arbitrate disagreements and, when necessary, to decide issues. Otherwise, the best that can be hoped for is half-hearted compromise with few positive results.

A certain amount of eccentricity is, for all that, essential to progress—unless, indeed, "progress" is defined as mere forward motion like the trundling of a streetcar. Eccentricity too, however, requires coordination in any group effort. Otherwise it can cause confusion.

An example of eccentricity is the typical artist, who generally works alone and seeks his inspiration within himself. Even in centuries when great art flourished,[*] however, there was perceived a need to make concessions to broader realities. The flowering of great art often coincided with times when the rules governing artistic expression were not only definite but, sometimes, even rigid. An example of extreme rigidity occurred under Islam, which completely forbade artists to imitate anything in nature. As Muslims, they had to content themselves with creating intricate geometric patterns and designs. This, however, they did with amazing versatility, beauty, and grace.

Nature, so far as I am aware, gives us no model of successful anarchy. As life evolved to the level of intelligent interaction, the need emerged for leadership. In any group, some guidance is necessary. A leader needn't have any other talent: All that he or she needs is a gift for coordinating and inspiring others. Leadership is a skill, simply, like painting or music composition or an aptitude for business. Part of the skill of leadership lies in knowing how to present an idea so that people will nod their heads instead of shaking them—and shaking their fists as well! Often, leadership skill depends on recognizing that there is truth on more than one side of an issue. It lies also in seeing that what everyone really wants may essentially be the same thing. The skill, in such cases, lies in being able to define an issue in such a

---

*Not the present time, unfortunately. Today's artist believes so firmly in freedom of self-expression that, sometimes, he may feel validated most completely when he has managed to give the greatest offense!

way as to be acceptable to all.

Leadership, then, is obviously essential in cooperative communities. If experiments in this direction have failed, it is largely due to some inadequacy in leadership. It takes a good leader to steer people to a harmonious conclusion. Groups that insist on spontaneous consensus achieve only low-energy decisions—arrived at, usually, after endless discussion. People are so exhausted in the end that they'll agree to almost anything, simply to get the talking over and done with.

How to explain what I mean by adequacy in leadership? The first thing a leader needs is to respect others as individuals. If he fails in this regard, it probably means he hasn't much respect for himself, either. His leadership style gets caught, consequently, in a tangle of self-consciousness, self-doubt, and compensatory bluster. Any attempt to help him out of this maze soon reveals to what extent leadership is a gift, not merely a position. It is a skill also, however, and as such can be learned in time, provided people are interested in self-correction.

Effective leadership is magnetic. The magnetism, however, should be of the right kind. For people can be guided foolishly as well as wisely. A leader may overwhelm others by the sheer force of his own opinions. He may intimidate others with his excessive confidence, feeling his own position to be unassailable. Or, again, he may seek to include others, and expect the best of them. This last type of leadership is suitable for cooperative communities, in which people come together for a life of inner freedom, harmony, and happiness.

Many of the ideas expressed below appear also in a book of mine, *The Art of Supportive Leadership.* * This book has been bought in quantity by several major corporations in America including Kellogg, Mitsubishi, and AT&T for distribution to their managers. It sells well, for the principles it presents have been tested and developed in actual practice. In this chapter I will suggest a number of new principles also.

First, it may aid understanding if I contrast this approach to the worst counsel that I know for rulers of nations, and for group leaders. That advice was written by Nicolò Machiavelli in his book, *The Prince*. Machiavelli's name has become synonymous with utter lack of scruples in the quest for power. I should mention at the outset that his advice has never, in the long term, been validated. Whatever success it has inspired has been temporary. Meanwhile, however, his teachings have inflicted untold misery.

The greatest flaw in Machiavelli's theories, however, is not even the misery they've inflicted. It is that they've encouraged rulers to go against their own nature, as human beings. Thus, they've created misery for the rulers themselves. In other words,

*Crystal Clarity Publishers, Nevada City, California (1987).

his counsel has proved a disaster for the very people he was trying to help. With Machiavelli to guide them, they needn't have worried about hell after death: He showed them how to create hell right here on earth. Whatever benefit may be derived from his teachings—I don't suggest that anyone bother to familiarize himself with them!—is that, *by contrast*, they show what is needed in a good leader.

Machiavelli (1469–1527) lived during the height of the Italian Renaissance. His books were written for rulers, not for commoners. According to him, the ordinary canons of morality, applicable to lesser human beings, are not valid for heads of state, whose goal should be to gain and hold absolute power.

In *The Prince* (*Il Principe*), written in 1513, Machiavelli attempted to justify every possible villainy—including treachery, torture, and murder—with the cold-blooded explanation that a ruler must do what is necessary to maintain his position. Modern businessmen, too, if they aren't overburdened with a conscience, seek similar justification. After bankrupting their competitors, they explain that action dismissively with the statement, "Business is business." Other people, too, use similarly specious arguments to excuse deeds they know instinctively to be wrong. And so it is that, for a certain kind of person, Machiavelli's book has been for centuries a veritable "bible" of success.

A number of writers, wanting to be fair, defend

Machiavelli with the claim that he wasn't really evil; that he was a republican at heart, and dreamed of living to see Italy united. It doesn't really matter what the fellow was like, personally. He may have had better intentions than his writings indicate. On the other hand, he may have been, as many believe, a devil. Machiavelli the man isn't at issue here. It is his teachings we are dealing with. In that context, Machiavelli is only a footnote.

The issue before us is this: Can human values legitimately be suspended in the case of rulers? Obviously, for starters, a prince doesn't have a different anatomical structure from lesser citizens. Nor has he a different mental or spiritual make-up. His tastes, appetites, and emotional needs require fulfillment like the rest of us.

The ancient Greeks and Romans invented myths in which gods and goddesses behaved as though they were above ordinary morality. One suspects those myths were allegories, created to accommodate the understanding of ordinary human beings, with the hope that in time they would find deeper meaning in them as the stories were told and retold many times. In any case, human beings are not gods, even if rulers have been known to order their subjects to treat them as such. Moral principles apply as much to kings as to beggars. Indeed, sometimes they apply even more so, for a beggar may be unaware of subtleties that ought to be obvious to a king.

Are certain *actions,* then, justified in a ruler that would not be so in his subjects? Can the rightness of an act be divorced from the well-being of him who acts, and from the well-being of those *for whom* he acts? Only its benefit to human beings can truly justify human behavior. And if well-being is accepted as a guideline, is it not as much so for the subjects as for the ruler? Is there any act that might, in itself, be justified in a ruler that would not be justifiable for ordinary citizens?

An example springs to mind: warfare. Sometimes war is necessary. In that sense, it is right. Defensive war, for example, may be the only way to protect a nation. Murder, however, is an act committed by individuals and can virtually never be justified. The decision to go to war must be made by rulers, not by common citizens. Even here, however, exceptions are imaginable. What if a madman enters a village and begins shooting everyone in sight? Wouldn't the villagers be morally right even to shoot him, if necessary, to save the entire village from becoming slaughtered?

Mahatma Gandhi, the renowned champion of non-violence, skirted this issue once when the question was put to him. "I would offer myself to be killed first," he replied. A beautiful answer, of course, but it wasn't properly responsive to the question. For what if that madman, after killing Gandhi, had continued on his rampage through the village? Wouldn't Gandhi's sacrifice in that case have seemed irresponsible—even a little bit foolish? In real life, bad choices must sometimes be made in preference to even worse ones. Moral issues cannot be determined absolutely. Everything in this world is, necessarily, relative.

An action is effective that accomplishes its objective. If, however, what it accomplishes is self-defeating and leads only to disappointment in the end, it cannot be termed a genuine success. Repeated disappointments in life persuade one at last that the long-range goal of all striving is not mere pleasure, acquisition, and worldly power, but things intangible: happiness, inner peace, and wisdom. If, indeed—as seems obvious—everyone's goal is his own fulfillment, we must ask ourselves also, when contemplating a course of action, Will it give me what I *really* want? Is it, from that standpoint, *meritorious*? that is, will it promote my own true well-being, and that of others? And can such well-being actually be purchased at the price of anyone else's?

Truth is truth. Honor is honor. There may be mitigating factors too subtle for most rulers to understand, but at every crossroads in life one can only be guided by one's own best understanding. A safe rule is this: Be true to what you feel in your heart to be the right course. Even so, you should keep yourself open to the possibility of a new direction, should one seem preferable in time. If the facts so indicate, one shouldn't hesitate to accept the change. Nor should one be concerned lest others see him as having lost face. It is no shame in a leader to accept the truth, whatever it may be, once recognition of the need for it dawns as events unfold. Truth alone, always, should be our guide.

It is sometimes good to have a "worst-case scenario." Let us ask ourselves, How much would we be willing to sacrifice for a clear conscience? One ought to be ready to give even life itself for a principle. Unless and until one is inwardly confident that he can embrace this choice, he will never be completely at peace inwardly. The fear of death, if of nothing else, will always loom over him like a dark cloud.

The following story is for those who face crucial decisions of conscience:

In a concentration camp during World War II, a number of Jews were brought to the camp commandant's office. He showed them the view through the glass window of his office door. "You see that gate across the courtyard from here?" he asked. "It is your gateway to freedom. I ask of you only this: As the condition for your release, you must renounce your Jewish faith."

With but one exception, every Jew in the room accepted his condition. They may have told themselves that, under such circumstances, apostasy would be no sin, and that their words of denial could be retracted later anyway, as having been made under duress. The commandant opened the door, and they hurried out toward the gate. As they were crossing the yard, they were all machine-gunned to death.

The sadistic commandant then turned to the one remaining Jew. "They were trash anyway," he remarked dismissively. "Of what good are people if they can't be faithful to a commitment of conscience?"

There are almost as many kinds of leadership as there are human beings. No sweeping system should be, or even could be, suggested for all. Forced efforts are unnatural, and can lead to disastrous results. Let us rather consider those who lead discriminating individuals, people whose conscience is free, who aren't concerned with the opinions of others, and who are willing honestly to seek a better way of life.

The only one suitable to lead people who are free in this way is one who respects them *as individuals*. No leader will meet this qualification if he tries to persuade others against their will, even if he is convinced that he desires only their well-being. Since he, like each of them, is an individual, he must respect above all their right to form their own judgment, even if he considers it to be wrong.

A leader should *lead* others, not drive them. He should inspire them to *want* to behave rightly. Indeed, a motto for enlightened leaders should be, *"People are more important than things."*

The ideas here presented are for this kind of

leader. They will help everyone, however, because all men find themselves, occasionally, in a position of having to make decisions for others. I present them generally, therefore, and don't plan to raise the bar so high that few can jump over it.

Here, to start with, is an essential guide: Before making a decision, don't ask only, "Will this plan advance the project?" Ask also, "Will it help me and all of us toward our fulfillment *as human beings*? Is there a danger that it may hinder that fulfillment?" Ask also, "Will it help us to develop *character*?" For character, it should be emphasized, is essential to genuine well-being.

It sometimes happens, for example, that sternness suggests itself as necessary for handling a situation. Ask yourself in this case, "How would it affect me, personally, to be stern? Could I act that way without losing my inner peace? Would I be able, in spite of being stern, to retain my friendship for them? Would I be able to remain sensitive to their needs? Or would I become caught in the grip of my own displeasure?" When ends are sought by the expression of harmful attitudes such as anger, one loses sight of the end in dust clouds of disharmony that are kicked up in the process. Sometimes the sacrifice must be made, but in this case one should do his best at least to be impersonal. He should expand his sense of self-identity to reduce his ego's involvement.

This principle holds true in every situation.

What determines the rightness of an action, ultimately, is its effect on the one committing it, and not only (as might be expected) on those toward whom the action is directed. No action, moreover, is an incident dangling in empty space, so to speak. It represents a commitment of energy, which becomes then a direction of movement. Consonant with Newton's first law of motion, energy wrongly directed can only be redirected, or blocked by a new and differently directed energy. Otherwise it will continue, reinforced by the will. In the normal course of events, sternness hardens to harshness, then to self-righteousness, and then to arrogance— unless from the beginning the ego is disengaged, or else is engaged from motives of kindness and good will, not of anger. The first question a leader should ask himself before every act ought to be, "What effect will this action have *on me?*" If it is likely to damage him, it is certain in some way to mar the deed itself.

Leaders would be wise to reflect on what a child I knew declared once after running a race. "Did you win?" he was asked. "No," he replied, "but I won against myself!" The best victories are those, always, which bring us greater clarity and inner strength.

Leadership is simply a job, in this respect neither more nor less important than any other. One person may be a tailor, another a merchant, a third a mountain guide. Skill at one's métier—in this case, leadership—is essential. Nevertheless, skill is nothing but a question of technique. To paint skillfully is not, in itself, to ensure that the work will be great. Infinitely more important is inspiration. Inspiration too, then, is important for good leadership. Moreover (returning to Machiavelli), there is no inspiration in cruelty, cunning, and ruthless oppression.

Again, whereas the pigment employed in portraying a human being can only suggest outwardly the nuances of his thinking, it is not in itself conscious. A ruler's subjects, on the other hand, *are* conscious. Whatever joy or suffering he imposes on them will return to him consciously also, and will either give him greater happiness or become a ball and chain on his conscience.

Rulers of nations and all leaders of groups must realize that their job is different, in this respect, from painting, or tailoring, or even playing chess. Leadership is not the manipulation of inanimate pawns, which all look alike, function alike, and have the same value in the game. Human beings are each, in some way, unique. They have names, personalities, facial features, bodily shapes, needs, likes and dislikes. Each of them, as a human being, deserves the respect of his social superiors that they give to their social equals. Wise is that leader who sees his job as a service to others, not as an opportunity to receive service from them.

Pride of position is an ugly defect in a leader.

Humility, on the other hand, is an ornament. Humility does not mean self-deprecation, which paralyzes the will. Humility means self-forgetfulness in concentration on the greater issues. Humility, in this sense, is the surest key to success in all things. Pettiness, on the other hand—the habit, for example, of losing one's temper, or of hurting others out of spite—costs more in the long run than any consequent gain.

The effects of action can seldom be predicted with certainty. Who knows what unexpected obstacles may arise? The one sure guide to right action, therefore, is to consider its probable effect *on oneself*, and on others, too, *as individuals*. Never look upon anyone as a mere cog in the wheel of progress, as though he had no individuality of his own.

Does a proposal promise significant *inner* gains? Does it offer increased self-assurance, strength, understanding, happiness, wisdom, inner peace? These results cannot easily be determined in advance. Often they can be perceived, however, by simply thinking an act through to its probable conclusion. In this sluggish material world, it takes time to see tangible results. The probable results of a course of action, however, can be perceived immediately, simply by imagining the *feeling* that is likely to accompany, or to ensue from, the proposed action. Is that feeling expansive, or contractive? If it is expansive, and if it conveys a sense of inner freedom, and, to others, a sense of sympathy, the proposal is likely to be good. It promises fulfillment. But if the feeling is contractive and causes one to withdraw one's sympathy from others, or to harden the consciousness of one's own importance, it presages disappointment. A contractive reaction in the contemplation of a course of action creates ripples of inner uneasiness. An expansive reaction, on the other hand, brings inner calmness. Be guided by these subtle indicators.

A ruler may occasionally have to make serious decisions that others will never face on their own. He should be guided always by these same considerations. Courage is more admirable than excessive caution, whether in one person or in many. And bullies usually respect courage, whereas they'll take full advantage of the coward. Pragmatic wisdom in leadership—a recognition, for example, of the need to compromise, occasionally; to bide one's time before making decisions that involve the well-being of many; to form occasional alliances of convenience: These things cannot always be avoided. Differences do exist, obviously, between the decisions one must make on behalf of others and those one might make for oneself.

A leader may be willing to renounce something personally, for example, that he would never surrender on behalf of other people: benefits, perhaps, that to him would be meaningless, but that to others might be vitally important. Every human reality has its own inherent needs and challenges. Football players require a different set of responses from those required in a statesman. Nevertheless, if a ruler, or a leader of others, is true to himself and to the highest expectations he holds of himself, he will be better guided than he ever would be by following the advice of cynics like Nicolò Machiavelli.

Whether Machiavelli was evil must be dismissed as more his business than our own. What is central to this discussion is whether his teachings work. Have they ever done so? His best-known book, *The Prince,* was the favorite reading of some of history's greatest villains. Oliver Cromwell, we are told, applied those principles to the Commonwealth government in England. Henry II and Henry IV of France were carrying copies of *The Prince* when they were murdered. (Might their interest in that book suggest the reason they met that fate?) An annotated copy of *The Prince* was found in Napoleon Bonaparte's coach at Waterloo. Adolf Hitler kept a copy of it by his bedside. And Benito Mussolini stated, "I believe *The Prince,* by Machiavelli, to be the statesman's supreme guide." Robert B. Downs, in *Books That Changed the World,* wrote, "Later, Mussolini changed his mind, for in 1939, on the list of authors, ancient and modern, placed on the Fascist index of books which Roman librarians must not circulate appeared the name Machiavelli." Surely Downs was being naive! If Mussolini decided he didn't want anyone reading that book after all, isn't it more likely he didn't want people to discover his own secrets?

The strongest case against Machiavelli is that his methods simply haven't shown themselves, in the long run, to work. A ruler may succeed in holding people in bondage for years by following Machiavelli's advice. He may, as *The Prince* recommends, make himself more feared than loved. When people's fear turns to hatred, however, they'll discount even the risks of taking revenge.

Machiavelli's teaching is self-annihilating, not self-exalting. Cromwell, Napoleon, Hitler, Mussolini, and other disciples of his won no laurels of victory in the end, but only the blunt, heavy ax of defeat.

The real benefit to be derived from reading Machiavelli is that he gives such clear lessons in what a ruler ought *not* to do if he aspires to rule well. When it is understood that true fulfillment lies within, not in outward achievements, it is understood also, by projection, where fulfillment lies for the body politic: not in trumpeted victories, but in the well-being of everyone, whether individually or in the millions.

The value of democracy, as opposed to government by kings and princes, is that democracy at least is designed on the principle of self-rule. Though it can be manipulative in practice, its accepted goal is the well-being of all. Citizens in a democracy are encouraged not to compete over how much of the pie each can grab for himself.

Truth, which should be the guiding principle for everyone, and therefore for every government, should be especially so in a democracy. Truth seldom springs, however, from hastily formed opinions. On this point democracies, especially, can fail, for they tend to be influenced by emotions of the moment, to the detriment of wisdom.

A leader should keep his heart's feelings unaffected by the shouts, plaudits, and hisses of the crowd. He should seek guidance calmly within himself and in consultation with those he considers wise rather than only politically savvy. He should never act under the influence of emotion, but should seek guidance in a broader vision. He should ask himself, "Toward what does our national conscience really aspire?" On the other hand, he cannot afford to outdistance by too far the values of the people he governs.

If the representative of a democratic people cannot stand by his own perception of the truth; or if he tells himself, "Who am I, after all? Just one voter, among so many!" he is not a true representative, and is not fit to rule. His duty is to condense in himself the conscience of those whom he has been called to serve.

True democracy is not achieved by mere ballot. It requires subtle recognition of the *deeper, long-term* will of the people, and a sensitive response to that will. Opinion polls rarely disclose that deeper impulse; the questions they ask are necessarily simplistic. Few people are able to verbalize their ideas clearly. Few even recognize what their ideas really are, until someone gives clear expression to them. A good leader listens calmly, and never tries to coerce anyone into accepting his ideas. He may, however, and indeed ought to, do his best to present his ideas persuasively. Certainly he should never resort to cunning in order to win people. He should not, for example, when proposing a project, withhold information that he knows might prejudice people against it. And he should not tell only that side of a story which he thinks will win people. He might succeed in getting away with tactics like these for a time, but people eventually will see what he is doing, and will cease to trust him. In short, he should not on any account use the methods Machiavelli recommended as necessary for a ruler.

Intelligence need not imply guilefulness. If, however, people oppose you cunningly, when all you want is the general good, don't flinch from opposing them with similar skill. To do so may mean using what one might call "kindly cunning," but it will spring only from a recognition that, in this world of relativities, one must accept the realities of others for what they are. Moreover, you should not parade your intentions too openly before those who are cunning, out of your own fondness for candor. Whereas it is good to be simple-hearted, don't be a simpleton!

This caution is especially important when dealing with an enemy power. As, when dueling with a sword, different techniques are required from those employed in boxing or, for that matter, in friendly conversation, so do the realities of confrontation with an enemy differ from those of communication with a friendly power, and of cooperation with it. If skillful tactics can be used honorably in dealing with a bully nation, it would be naive not to use them, for in such cases one has no choice but to meet their fire with fire of one's own. If, however, it is your enemy's way to fight frankly and openly, then meet him in a kindred spirit. Only when an enemy fights underhandedly should his methods be turned against him. For example, if you learn that he is secretly inciting people against you, telling them that you have been skirting certain important issues, bring those issues immediately out into the open. Announce publicly, "These are serious problems. What shall we all do about them?" In this way, you'll take the wind out of their sails, and place the responsibility for solving the issues on everybody's shoulders, including those of your detractors.

Never, in any event, resort to underhanded methods yourself. An unscrupulous enemy will not think you capable of anything but deceit anyway. Let him deceive himself, if he so chooses. Don't be untruthful, but if he chooses to think you guileful, let him be hoist by his own petard. Above all, be honest with yourself. If you find it necessary to equivocate—for instance, if you send the message,

"The winters in our country are mild," when in fact this particular winter happens to be unusually harsh, but favorable to your country's impending struggle against an invader—be satisfied within yourself that, still, you have told the truth.

A rule for lasting success may be stated as follows: *Adherence to high principles gives the only certainty there is of final victory.*

An intelligent leader works with people as they are, not as he may wish they were or think they ought to be. An intelligent, *good* leader seeks the highest good for all—for his foes as well, if his heart is broad enough to include them too, in his sympathies. An intelligent but *bad* leader, however, seeks only personal gain.

Ask yourself, *Cui bono*—Who stands to gain: the leader, or the people he leads? If he seeks nothing for himself (be grateful that such people do exist), don't be surprised if he is hated by people with small minds and desiccated hearts.

The above principles, rather than any mere sampling of public opinion, define that kind of democracy in which the people are guided by honor, not by guile. For if a leader gives people merely what they are asking for, or what he thinks they want, or even what they themselves are shouting vociferously that they want but will be disposed, later on, to reject in disappointment, his own is the true failure. He has failed in his duty, first of all, to himself. And he has failed in his duty to those whom he should be guiding. His job is to honor the deeper, not the transient, "will of the people." If necessary, his duty is to save them from plunging off a cliff they haven't seen.

Machiavelli verbalized—and at least he did so with more ruthless honesty than many—a philosophy of government that has, in fact, prevailed secretly for unnumbered centuries. In history there have been many Hitlers, Stalins, and Mao Tsetungs on scales both large and small. We may hope that people nowadays understand these things better than they used to. Given the alternative between self-fulfillment and universal misery, few today—so one hopes—would opt for misery.

Of course, a nation gets the kind of ruler it deserves. In any hope for utopia, one can realistically expect nothing better than a compromise between the ideal and the actual human reality.

Reflecting on Machiavelli's teaching, anyone who would create a better society must realize that the goal of leadership cannot be other than the well-being of all—of others too, that is, as extensions of one's own self. The goal must not be power for its own sake. People's happiness, and their will to achieve it each one in his own way, should be the goal of every leader, whether of small groups or of a government.

It is unlikely that society will ever achieve perfection. There is a hope, however, that a few societies, at least, may be channeled in a better *direction,* and inspired to seek a truer fulfillment. With this improvement for a beginning, who knows how far the zephyrs of healing may not blow?

If there is one rule for the creation of a better society, it is that which I've stated already: *People are more important than things*. The "things" implied here include systems, projects of all kinds, and occasionally, even, time-worn rules and traditions. For there are times when tradition, even when cherished, must be ignored. A leader must consider every situation in itself. He must not say, "Well, in situations like this, here is what we are accustomed to doing." If necessary, he must be ready to depart from solutions that have worked before.

Human beings cannot be forced into ideational straitjackets. In the ancient Greek story of Theseus, the villain Procrustes, whom Theseus slew, offered a special bed to his guests. Pretending to offer them a good night's rest, he would ask them to lie down, then strap them forcibly onto the bed. If their legs were too long, he lopped them off, leaving them to bleed to death. If their legs were too short, he stretched their bodies to make them fit, laughing as they died in agony.

Machiavelli proposed no utopian system, certainly, but the means he proposed for manipulating people have tempted many rulers to behave like Procrustes. Following Machiavelli's advice, or simply drinking from the same polluted stream he did, they have embraced the time-dishonored doctrine, "The end justifies the means."

In the last analysis—how strange it is to contemplate it!—his system reflected a delusion not so very different from one that utopian writers have proposed: that mere systems are capable of regulating human existence.

Love alone is the power that people will accept wholeheartedly. Not force, and not mathematically precise planning. Love, or at least sincere respect, is the secret of true success in a leader. Love alone can lead to a better life on earth. I don't mean personal love, which practices favoritism and encourages toadyism, but love above all for truth, and especially for the truth that resides in all beings. Love is a force that few social philosophers have ever taken into consideration. In Machiavelli's unsentimental disdain for fellow-feeling he failed to appreciate this far superior power. His own heart was a desert where no wildflowers of love bloomed.

Life, according to accepted theory nowadays, is a product of random material interactions. Consciousness also—again, according to accepted theory—is the product of the mere movement of energy in a circuit of brain cells. Mechanisms are believed to explain everything.

As we proceed in the following pages, however, we shall see that life and consciousness are no mere consequence, but are the subtle cause of everything man can ever know.

CHAPTER FOUR

❋

Ask First: Will It Work?

It is astonishing the degree to which intelligent people, especially intellectuals and academics, seem willing to accept theories in place of reality. We have seen in the case of Machiavelli that his theories have never worked in practice, except temporarily. Of the test cases we examined, all of them eventually lost their power. Napoleon Bonaparte spent the remainder of his life in exile on St. Helena. Hitler committed suicide. Mussolini was killed by an angry mob and hung head downward in Piazzale Loreto in Milan. The question doesn't merit an in-depth study, for no proof is needed, surely, to convince any sensible person that ruthless cruelty is bound to attract retribution in kind. The astonishing thing, as we've said, is that people with a fondness for theories can remain satisfied if a theory is expressed cleverly, even if it has been shown not to work. Sometimes, the theory itself is abhorrent to human nature: It doesn't seem to matter. Indeed, the more it defies common sense, the more it is embraced as a challenge to "scientific objectivity." Are people's egos flattered, merely, by the cleverness of the moves an author makes on his intellectual chessboard? Machiavelli basically a republican at heart? I ask you! As well stress that a Mafia capo can't really be considered criminal: After all, he's a loving grandfather to the handful of brats who bear his proud name.

Jean Paul Sartre was a case in point. I submitted his writings to lengthy analysis in a book of mine, *Out of the Labyrinth,** so will not repeat myself here except to say that as an intellectual and a philosopher he is a fraud. One example should suffice: Sartre based what was perhaps his most important argument on the declared but untested premise, "Man is radically free." After pages of intellectual dust which he threw into the reader's eyes, he concluded, "Therefore, man is radically free." This is *logic?*

Yet Sartre has been the darling of intellectuals for decades, not because what he writes rings true to anyone's experience, but because he states it so cleverly. He tries by trickery to persuade the reader that his case is plausible, until the reader begins to doubt his own reason. This is mental sleight-of-hand: The "magician" announces, "Let's just say— only for the sake of argument, mind you—that such-and-such is the case. Assuming it as a possibility—a *mere* possibility—here is what follows from it logically." Having continued in this line for paragraphs, pages, or a whole book, one finds oneself

*Crystal Clarity Publishers, Nevada City, California; third edition, revised and renamed 2001.

stumbling by dim candlelight in the dark, marveling at the "magician's" cleverness, and at last forgetting altogether that the foundation for this entire line of reasoning was the question, "What if?" To accept illogic "tentatively" is a path to error from which few find their way back.

Some people are reluctant to abandon an argument that is beautifully reasoned, even if they know, or once knew, that its foundation was made of sand. Today, Sartre enjoys less of a vogue than he once did, but his theories are still propounded vigorously by others as though they were their own.

Plato, in *The Republic,* proposed several unattractive prospects for what he considered the ideal political state. Because his ideas were elaborately thought out, and because, after all, he was Plato, his notions have been debated solemnly for over two thousand years, especially in university classrooms. His was the first known attempt to present a detailed plan for a "perfect" society.

Plato, like many since him, formulated a system that might, just conceivably, work. He then proposed that people be squeezed into that system, as Procrustes tried to do to his "guests," who must, he insisted, fit onto his bed. The most common mistake in utopian theory has always been the supposition that people's behavior can be determined radically by outward conditioning. The individual's own will in the matter is not even considered. This was B. F. Skinner's philosophy in his novel, *Walden Two*. Will it work? Well, it never has.

I really cannot believe that behaviorist psychologists, most of whom, presumably, have had children of their own, will be able to continue forever in the delusion—to them, it is a dogma—that environmental conditioning is the whole explanation for the diversity in people's natures. Environment is important, yes, but it is only one factor. The most obvious disproof of this modern dogma is that children are so widely varied from birth. Some of them have always shown a tendency to be positive. Others, quite the opposite: Their nature from the outset has been negative. Some are basically cheerful and courageous; others, dour, or timid, or expectant of the worst from others and from life. Siblings are often very unlike one another, and, again, quite different from their parents or from anyone among whom they've been raised. The behaviorist theory is not only contrary to common sense, but has never been demonstrated in action. It is all based on the same old question, "What if?"

"Let's just suppose," says the theorist. To that "suppose" I must reply, "Play your own games. I'm busy with ideas that at least show a promise of leading somewhere."

Perhaps the greatest mistake utopian writers have made is to presume that people's behavior can be both known in advance, and made to fit that prediction.

Vance Packard described psychological tests that were given to soldiers during World War II as a means of ascertaining which of them would make good commandos. In virtually every case, the results of those tests were no more accurate than if the selection had been made by blowing the test papers onto a staircase with a fan, after assigning a different value to each step. Men whose written tests gave an impression of resource and courage showed themselves to be deflated balloons under combat conditions; on the other hand, a number of those who had raised doubts that they might prove timid showed themselves under fire to be courageous, resourceful, and in some cases heroic.

Plato proposed that people be selected in early childhood for their role in life. Rulers, he said, should be chosen from the beginning for their natural wisdom, intellectual superiority, strength of character, unselfishness, disdain for luxury, and eagerness to serve the good of all. (Could all those traits reveal themselves in the nursery?) Those who served the rulers as "Guardians" must, again, be chosen while they were very young, since their education had to be determined well in advance. Such children would be submitted to rigorous, well-rounded mental, moral, and physical training. Their reading material was to be carefully screened to exclude even the poet Homer, who too-often represented the gods as weak and imperfect, and who, besides, overdramatized the human emotions. The music the children were allowed to hear must not be frivolous, and must therefore be carefully censored also.

The governing elite would live under a communistic system, sharing property, homes, and meals. People were to be allowed free entry into one another's homes. They would live together, eat together, and eschew as distracting to their public spirit any semblance of a family life. The leading classes of society were not permitted mates of their own, and any children they produced would be unknown to them as their own, nor would the children know their own parents. All were to be considered children of the state.

The more one ponders this mathematically exact but grotesque system, the more one is repelled. Interestingly, Plato's ideas remind one of some of the least attractive features of modern communism.

To keep our focus on Plato, however, the decisive question remains: Is his system workable? An interesting feature of his life, to which few, as far as I know, have paid much attention is that he actually conducted a test of his ideas. In the year 367 B.C. he was invited by Dionysius the Younger, ruler of Syracuse, to come and turn his kingdom into a utopia along the lines described in *The Republic*. Plato accepted. The experiment proved a fiasco.

Enough said? Surely, yes!

At least Plato's experiment was conducted on a

limited scale, rather than inflicted on reluctant millions. Communism, on the other hand, though intended to be the outcome of a spontaneous uprising of "the people," is one of the cruelest jokes ever to be endorsed by theory-addicted intellectuals. Karl Marx's theories looked good to those intellectuals, on paper. Perhaps they still look good to some of them. Written as a theory, the ideas seemed to many as though they ought to work, and therefore *must* work! If they didn't, it could only mean that people hadn't developed proper appreciation for them. Who, then, could blame the Bolsheviks and other communists for wiping out these misfits like faulty sentences on a page? As Ninotchka says in the movie of that name, after the purges "there will be fewer but better Russians."

Countless millions had to die to produce those "better Russians"—and, later on, those "better" Chinese, Cubans, Cambodians, and all the rest. The "intellectuals," however, have never lived to see victory for their theories. With every revolution, they've been the first ones to be eliminated, for their very intelligence posed a threat to the New Order. They, more than anyone else, would quickly realize what a monstrosity they had spawned, and would expose it.

Karl Marx said his theories were for the upliftment of "the masses." His so-called "dictatorship of the proletariat" was ushered in by a mere handful of revolutionaries, relatively speaking: five thousand people, in a country of many millions. Few of those revolutionaries were idealists; most of them were motivated not by noble sentiments, but by envy, rage, and hatred. Those who rose to the top, like scum on a pond, were the most ruthless of the lot: Machiavellian in practice even if few or none of them had read *The Prince*. Stalin—a Genghis Khan, truly—butchered all who stood in his way. His ambition was for power and for his own security and physical safety; certainly it wasn't to fulfill the "communist dream" discussed by many intellectuals in the fashionable clubs and universities of England and America. Stalin trampled underfoot the broken dreams of wishful thinkers, and of failed Machiavellians whose only "fault" was that they were, perhaps, less criminal than himself.

Marx was more motivated by bitterness against society than by concern for his fellowman. His entire system may be compared to a wineglass turned upside down: the bottom on the top, while the red liquid—blood, not wine—stains the tablecloth and the carpet underneath. Since Marx's day, the very definition of numerous words has been so distorted as to give a new meaning to concepts most of us cherish. "Progressive," for the modern communist, means regressive in normal terminology, since it is against true progress and amounts to enslaving people by making them dependent on factors outside themselves. "Truth" is whatever affirms communist doctrines (even if it is manifestly a lie). "Untruth" is anything that contradicts those doctrines. And "freedom" is security bestowed by the government; it is not the liberty to direct one's own life as one chooses.

Among concepts that have been twisted out of all recognition by communists are two more: *conservative* and *political sophistication.* "Conservative" doesn't mean to *conserve* values, but to react against the policies of supposedly "enlightened" regimes that impose their will—always a minority one—on a whole populace. "Political sophistication" means to be naive' enough to believe in theories that contradict universal human experience.

The basic difference between Plato and Marx was that Plato at least envisioned leaders who were concerned for the public well-being: men who were intelligent, wise, and in every way competent for the job. Plato assumed that there are heights toward which the human race can aspire. His "utopia" was a folly, of course, but at least it contained aspiration toward higher human potentials. Karl Marx, on the other hand, considered the manual laborer to be the best definition of humanity. To Marx, conditioned as he was by Darwin's theory of evolution, the animal essence in man *is* the reality.

Much modern literature describes this "basic human being," suggesting that those who aspire to selfless love, spirituality, kindness, and nobility are the victims of false notions, and are being simply dishonest with themselves.

"Dream Girl," a Broadway production several decades ago, made fun of a young woman who denied her basic animalism. Then a young man, lusting for her body though having little use for her soul, awakened her to life's "realities." The young man, the audience was led to believe, was a realist. The girl, high-minded and idealistic until her "awakening," lived in a dream world. Of course, the playwright was on the young man's side, and therefore had to make the girl appear just as foolish and impractical as his dramatic art allowed.

One simple example, though perhaps trivial in itself, speaks volumes for the lack of integrity in Marx's philosophy. The value of a commodity, he said, should be determined by the amount of labor that went into it. Others had proposed this notion before him—Adam Smith was a notable example. None, however, had put into that theory so much emotional fervor.

Viewing this notion with plain common sense, and leaving aside such practical matters as the cost of the machines involved and the cost of maintaining them, one must ask: If an untrained carpenter spends more time in making a house than a more experienced one, and if he makes it less suitable for living in, is his house even so worth more simply because he devoted more hours to its construction? Marx and other exponents of the "labor theory of value" sought to address this problem, speaking of an "abstract labor" that took such differences of skill into account. A person's training, experience, *and intelligence,* however, are crucial to the value of any contribution he makes to society.

Friedrich Engels, who eulogized Karl Marx at his funeral, said, "He discovered the simple fact, heretofore hidden beneath ideological overgrowths, that human beings must have food and drink, clothing and shelter, first of all." These needs, Marx said, determine everything else a man does. Do they also, then, determine the heights to which a human being can aspire? Aspiration itself, according to Marx's viewpoint, would be only a mask to hide lower animal impulses.

Even in the animal world, however, intelligence often counts for more than brute force. The stupid "hulk" who understands only brawn is in no way competent to guide society in its affairs. Marx's appeal to the lowest grade of mentality as the "cream" of humanity was a cruel hoax. All he did was appeal to people's envy, while deriding high aspirations as pretentious. The system he proposed implies that genius deserves to be penalized (unless harnessed in service to the state), and stupidity exalted. The fact is, of course, that rulers in every communist state have always been people with the guile to fool others into accepting slogans in place of the truth.

A friend of mine once wanted to bake a cake for

a wedding. She was an excellent cook. Still, thinking the occasion warranted something special, she tested her recipe on a few friends first, baking only a small cake. Receiving their approval, she had the confidence to bake a large cake for the festive event. Isn't it obvious that new social ideas, too, should be tested on a few people first, before being inflicted on many?

If a social philosophy works on a limited scale, it may work for the many. Even so, it would be sensible to test it further before making it universal. Murdering everyone who doesn't like it is, among other things, counter-productive. For it means to admit frankly that the theory is not for everybody. Of course, people theorize further that a perfect society, once it has been created, will *produce* perfect people. The theory crumbles, however, for two simple reasons: First, people are not mindless "products"; to varying degrees, they have intelligence. They can think for themselves, and only the dullest of them think as they've been told to. Second, a society built on murder will necessarily carry forward the murderous tendency. No society whose "comrades" never know which of them will be murdered next can have the inner security that comes with "social perfection."

No system can prove acceptable to everyone, for human nature is infinitely varied. Any social experiment, then, that is imposed wholesale on a large and heterogeneous group of people cannot successfully serve them all. The best that can be hoped for, rather, is that a few people may succeed in creating a better society, and that a few more, then, seeing the idea in action, will be inspired to try it.

"Example speaks louder than words." No idea can be imposed on people by force. If, however, a few can be inspired to embrace it, perhaps others will be similarly moved. Only thus, like an expanding light, may a great change take place that could affect the very course of history.

CHAPTER FIVE

❋

Living Things Begin Small

Is it necessary for untold millions to suffer and die in order for grand social theorists like Marx and Machiavelli to be proved wrong? In the last chapter we asked the simple, even obvious, question: Will it work? A corollary to that question is: Has it been tried? And a third one, no less obvious: Was it first tried on a small, *manageable* scale? Communism certainly was not.

In reading social theories, one cannot fail to be struck by the general deficiency in their formulators' understanding of human nature. Even Plato didn't pay much attention to individual human beings with their special characteristics, interests, and ambitions. Rather, he treated them all as stereotypes, and imagined destinies determined for them by a "wise" government. Shall one person be told, "Be an artist"? and another, "Be a farmer"? Shall this one be ordered, "Be wise!" and that one, "Be foolish!"? People simply are what they are; they cannot be designed according to the demands of social theory.

To develop insight into humanity as a whole, one must begin with the individual. Indeed, the first person needing to be studied is one's self. To lump people together like so many snowflakes in a ball is to deny their individuality, and thereby to deprive them of their humanity. Most of the major developments in history have been initiated by individuals with the courage to think for themselves. Even group developments have required the unifying influence of a leader. As Emerson put it, "An institution is the lengthened shadow of one man."

Living things begin small. The Christian religion was started by one person: Jesus Christ. Since then, Christianity's greatest influence has been on the conscience of the individual, not on amorphous masses of people. Mass conversions are emotional and can only, therefore, be superficial. Only a person whose conscience is committed to a new concept is able to embrace it with sensitive perception. In religion, mass conversions are a travesty. In politics, mass movements more often bring chaos than clarity. In Christian history, perhaps the most unfortunate event with major consequences was when Emperor Constantine, in the early fourth century, decreed Christianity as the new state religion. Calm focus, not diffusion, is the key to all meaningful development. Without it, clarity is never achieved.

Meaningful development resembles the expanding, concentric rings in a tree trunk. Life's growth begins always at its center. By contrast, a work of sculpture, though it resemble a living creature, is nothing but chiseled stone. Nylon threads differ from plant fiber in the fact that there is no hole down the center of them for the life-force to pass through.

Pygmalion, in Greek legend, sculpted a statue of a woman so beautiful that he fell in love with it. He prayed that she be given life, and his prayer was granted: The statue became the woman, Galatea.* Art alone, however, hasn't the power to bestow life. To make it even seem alive, some sort of "grace," or sensitive perceptivity, is needed. Artists are obliged to approach their work from outside. Only the great artist is able to project some of his own essence into his creations, and to produce thereby a suggestion, at least, of Pygmalion's miracle. Most artists can do no more than imitate appearances.

Communities have been proposed as though they were stone sculptures: The projections are artificial. As in badly written novels, the characters of which act as the plot dictates instead of as the people's nature indicates, the characters in most communitarian dreams are not self-animated. In real life those communities would be doomed to failure. Plato's experiment in Syracuse was a flop. No community could succeed if its every decision

---

*This name may be apocryphal. For the modern playgoer, the name Eliza Doolittle naturally springs to mind!

had to be referred back to some intellectualized "blueprint," instead of allowed to grow according to the people's actual nature.

People cannot be forced to act against that nature. A basic condition for cooperative intentional communities is respect for the individual. The secret of developing such communities is not to let their members stumble about on their own, but to coordinate them with sensitive regard to their individual natures. No one can be forced into embracing an idea. Many, however, can at least be inspired *in the direction* of that idea, especially if the person who inspires them views others as dear to him, rather than as outside the circle of his sympathies.

The leader of a community must also *live* what he preaches. It is not enough to justify himself with theoretical abstractions. One such abstraction often encountered nowadays is verbalized as "people power." Almost always the leader who proclaims, "Power to the people!" is really only trying to silence opposition to his own ideas. He thrives on hurling denunciations, which he declaims with angry emotion. Diatribes are not easily contradicted, for people who depend on common sense prefer to speak softly. Their voices may not be heard above the pandemonium.

Communism tries in its every slogan to appeal to "people power." Under that oppressive system, however, "the people" themselves are—as Joseph

Stalin put it—mere "statistics." "People power" is, in fact, "ego power" declared by a demagogue.

Democracy is another story, for people in a democracy *do* count for something. Everything is, or at least is supposed to be, for the general good.

One of the "magician's tricks" Karl Marx performed was to create the illusion that the true opposition is between communism and capitalism. It is not. Every enterprise requires capital, whether the money comes from business investors or from a government. Communism merely seizes people's capital and pretends, in the name of "the people," to be managing their affairs. Since politicians are not inclined by either necessity or nature to be experts on profit and loss, they usually manage such affairs badly, and rarely to anyone's advantage but their own. Meanwhile, the real contrast of communism to other systems has always been between absolute rule, for their own selfish good, by a few (oligarchy) and rule for the sake of the many (democracy).

Nevertheless, to expect anything great and lasting to be brought about through mass initiative remains a delusion. In mass movements, it is emotions that rule. And emotions rise and fall constantly, like ocean waves. Often, once they've reached a peak, they crash heavily, causing destruction. Such were the mobs during the French Revolution, who destroyed indiscriminately but raised nothing in place of what they had overthrown. It took Napoleon, finally, to give the French Revolution some sort of focus.

"Citizens!" "Comrades!" "Friends, Romans, countrymen!": What do words like these really mean? Nothing. They are uttered, supposedly, in affirmation of solidarity, but in fact they are only promotional gimmicks intended to capture the imagination of emotionally immature people. Cassius, in Shakespeare's play "Julius Caesar," addressed the Romans with the last of those phrases, then contradicted the sentiment only moments later. Often, indeed, when people begin with flattery it is to end with criticism.

Mass movements are of their very nature emotional. The intellect, without aid from the emotions, lacks motive force. It can only analyze. It is an armchair traveler. The feeling quality is required, to give momentum to thought. *Emotional* feelings, however, tend in the long run to be disruptive, even if they begin with positive intentions.

Inspired feeling, on the other hand, is of a very different sort. Like a seagull, it transcends the rising and falling waves of emotion. Inspired feeling is rooted in calmness, which, united to balanced reason, is what it takes to bring about constructive results. Calm inspiration is responsible for every great work in history, whether in the arts, in philosophy, in science, or in politics.

Mass emotion finds its epitome in lynch mobs howling for vengeance. The individuals in those crowds might never consider violence were they acting on their own. Mass emotion, however, once awakened, exercises a hypnotic influence. The only hope of a mob being guided wisely is if someone emotionally uninvolved flows first with the tide, then steers the excitement gradually toward some wholesome end.

An example of this technique is shown in the story of a French mob that once stormed a jail, certain that an inmate there was guilty of some heinous crime. Loudly they demanded summary "justice"—that is to say, an immediate execution. The policeman in charge, a man of stolid common sense, stood before them on the front steps and shouted above their cries:

"Well done, citizens! Your demonstration shows the will of the people! I congratulate you for your courage! Justice, I promise you, shall now be done! Return to your homes, proud of being French, with a Frenchman's dedication to French honor! Again I say it, Thank you! Thank you! . . . and, our Republic also thanks you!" The mob disbanded, cheering lustily. As things turned out in the end, the prisoner was acquitted of all wrongdoing.

The best thing to emerge from mob emotion, usually, is the shout, "*Somebody* ought to *do* something!" The worst is wanton rampage and ruin. Midway between devastation and common sense are the harmless, but bizarre, manias that sometimes seize people, like one during the Middle Ages that sent crowds of people running about the countryside in packs, howling like wolves.

The problem with swallowing the emetic of "people power" is that the greater an emotion, the more difficult it is for it to return to calmness. People in their excitement are not swayed except by further excitement. Angry rhetoric stirs them, but reason? rarely! The very music they enjoy contains shrieking and a pounding beat designed to inflame their emotions. Soothing music, because healing to body and mind, they dismiss as "not where it's at, man!" Consider the statement a young woman made whose job was in a radio station where "heavy metal" music was played constantly. She was related to a friend of mine, and in that capacity had joined me and others for dinner in a restaurant. She told us about some of the violent attitudes the musicians displayed who came to the studio. Curious, I asked her what she thought of Mozart. "Mozart!" she cried disdainfully. "He's *dead!*" (Was she by comparison, I wondered, so very much alive?)

It isn't that people are sheep. Far from it. Most of them aren't stupid. It is, indeed, gratifying to sound them out and find how often they offer good suggestions, either supportive to an idea or as a corrective to it. It is only that few of them will initiate new ideas themselves. Most of them, besides, are not skilled at verbalizing their ideas. The best way to draw them out is on a one-on-one basis. In gatherings, the best way is to offer a plan, rather than throwing out a general invitation to "someone" to suggest something. Creativity is not a trait many people possess, but the ability to *improve* on suggestions is fairly common. From this ability, their creativity can be developed.

I say these things not theoretically, but based on years of personal experience, during which my work has been with intelligent people, not morons. Even minds that are unaccustomed to deep thought may possess a latent gift of insight if they are encouraged, and once their interest has been awakened. The important thing is to stir that interest, and then to listen to them. It is wise also, if people oppose an idea, to drop it altogether as unfeasible at least for the time being. For opposition may muddy the clearest stream, whereas, if it is given time to settle, it may actually enhance clarity.

This is practical, as opposed to theoretical, democracy. Theoretical democracy vaunts the populist dogma, "The people know best." In fact, the people seldom do. When they actually do know best, it is when a proposal is put to them simply, briefly, logically, and with crystal clarity.

Essentially, people are more problem-conscious than solution-conscious. Problems have a way of crowding every other possibility out of their consideration. A good leader must be solution-oriented. He must focus on what will work, not on the obstacles in the way to making it work. A further, and fascinating, fact is that solution-consciousness actually *attracts* to itself right answers, whereas problem-consciousness prevents answers from even arising in the mind.

Whether an issue involves a small group of people or a whole nation, leaderless democracy simply won't work—unless, indeed, the issues under consideration are trivial and the solutions to them more or less obvious. Consensus works well enough in situations where no commitment of energy is needed. Confronted with serious decisions, however, a good leader never imposes his will on others. Instead, he listens to them, and hears those especially who keep to the point instead of rambling on to no purpose. Of course, if he is the captain in a battle he may have no choice but to demand of those under him that they risk their lives. In such a case, he should try to emphasize a higher good. He should also take pains to offset the demands he makes of others by making equally uncompromising demands of himself.

Solution-consciousness requires focused energy. If a vote is required, the leader should phrase the resolution in such a way as to *invite,* rather than command, agreement. If a significant faction disagree, he should invite everyone to think about the matter further, in private if possible rather than in emotion-charged "forums." If a decision is urgently required, however, he must be guided by inner calmness, and accept responsibility for whatever decision is reached.

At a certain point, the time passes for further deliberation. Energy must then be directed toward implementing the decision, whatever it is. Otherwise the "Hamlet complex" sets in, causing endless indecision and delay.

The most important consideration in the decision-making process is to realize that truth cannot be voted into existence. Truth simply *is.* To find it, what is needed is calm insight, not ripples of likes, dislikes, and opinions. Usually it takes a single person to perceive a solution. If more than one perceive it, all the better. If a thousand people perceive it, wonderful. What usually happens, however, is that those thousand only endorse what is put before them convincingly.

"What shall we do?" is the worst question a leader can ask at the start of a meeting, unless he already knows what needs to be done. To leave the question open is like inviting everyone to huddle together and invent a new flying machine. Inspiration always comes from within. To "brainstorm" an idea is useful primarily as a means of overcoming problem-consciousness. Inspiration, however, shines out from one's inner self. It is the only way to know for certain what path to follow. Often, this recognition brushes aside impatiently the scribbled list of brainstormed ideas.

If a community is to succeed, it must begin with one sincere person, backed by a few others who are dedicated to the same basic concept. Thereafter, ideas must be offered almost in the form of informal *invitations* to whoever seems compatible with them. Communities must begin small. They must draw into their center only those who respond voluntarily. To try to impose a system on reluctant millions would be to guarantee disaster. Those millions will only distort the best attempts, and cause them in the end to be mere reflections of their own desires.

Communism, imposed as it has been on whole nations, has never worked. The people of East Germany, for instance, once Germany was reunited, found great difficulty in reviving the creative initiative they'd shown decades earlier. They were so accustomed to a state of security as the accepted alternative to political freedom that they dreaded the independence now expected of them, even though challenged by their very integrity to show initiative.

Society today is in a state of flux. Everything seems confused: moral, artistic, and philosophic values, religious ideals, political principles. Surely there were times in history when small societies, at least, were inspired by high principles, and when greed and envy were not so pronounced as they are today. Earthly perfection may be an unrealistic dream, but is it wildly unrealistic to hope that at least something better may be achieved than what we have today? There is a great need for human betterment. I don't speak of betterment only in technology—something everyone expects—but of the quality of human life, and of the refinement of human consciousness. If there is hope that even a step can be taken in this direction, the only way I see to achieve it is through small groups of individuals. Nothing can be achieved by thousands of people fanatically committed to creating the *one,* the *only,* the *best* society. The best way can only be through small groups of people banding together and seeking a better way of life in little communities, sanely, and harmoniously.

Because of the sheer complexity of human nature, I don't suggest that people continue wasting energy dreaming of a perfect world. Perhaps one grows cynical, having seen the failure of so many grandiose schemes for social reformation. In any case, if it is possible to bring about even a slight improvement in the lives of a few people, much may be accomplished, someday, for humanity as a whole from their example. For now, there must be small beginnings. What this book may do is inspire a few people, not everybody, with the possibility of setting small examples of a better way of living. I am not referring to only one kind of community, but to a variety of them, each one a reflection of noble aspirations and high ideals.

A network of such small communities, each of them autonomous, spreading gradually over the earth, may inspire humanity everywhere to better ways of living. Such a concept, surely, is not unrealistic. I believe it is feasible.

CHAPTER SIX

❋

Adam Smith and the Principle of Laissez Faire

Wealth is traditionally identified with tangible property—land, cattle, and other material possessions—with money, and with intangible "goods" such as patents and copyrights. Is a person wealthy to the extent that he has those things? No, not unless he values them. Value, for each person, is a subjective consideration. Economists, however, treat it as an objective truth, and consider themselves to be working with a science as exact as physics or chemistry. (Does not everyone with the slightest claim to methodology today clamber onto the bandwagon of modern science?) Economists equate value with cost—the cost of production and distribution, of advertising, and of other objective factors—as determining the price of things. Price, to them, equals value.

Viewed subjectively, however, price has little to do with value. Value is the worth we personally place on a thing. Our view of wealth may be very different from that of an economist. In this chapter

I propose to take the subjective view, and I think you may end up agreeing that this one is more valid for someone who is concerned, not with how to become rich in terms of saleable possessions, but in terms of what one himself really values.

So far, I've been submitting traditional explanations for things, whether cosmic or mundane, to a re-evaluation based on common sense, and on a view that is more meaningful from a human perspective. For whereas the economists' explanations may be important for people whose concerns are more global, they may be useless for those whose interest lies in finding personal fulfillment, or for that matter for people with a broader spectrum of values than the concern for mere property.

Economists, of course, predicate their thinking on the assumption that, since a certain amount of material wealth is desirable, more of it is even more desirable. Material wealth, however, becomes highly *un*desirable once a person realizes that a surfeit of it results not in freedom, but in bondage. Why, indeed, should anyone join the stampede toward surfeit and suffering, if a sane alternative for attaining happiness exists, especially if that alternative doesn't mean self-deprivation? Why follow a road for no other reason than the fact that others travel it? Why not, instead, go by a more scenic route?

My concern in these pages has not been with mechanisms, but with meaning—meaning as it applies to us as human beings. From an economist's standpoint, it is pricing that is of interest, not values. The subject is extraordinarily complex, and becomes increasingly so the deeper one delves into it. To understand the subject fully may be impossible, for it soars into the reaches of higher mathematics where abstruse theory drifts off into unprovable conclusions and may lead in virtually any direction one fancies. That complexity is only technical, however. From a human point of view, the situation is relatively simple.

Clear light on the subject is needed, however, to illuminate it. One difficulty with economic theory is the notorious unreliability of its predictions.

A friend of mine in Australia, a successful financier, told me about a venture he'd once launched. After the first year, he said, the business showed a deficit. His accountants explained to him the reasons why.

"Could you have told me that at the beginning of the year?" he inquired. They admitted they could not have. "So," he said in conclusion, "I fired the lot of them. From that time on I let myself be guided by my own common sense, and the business flourished." He confessed he'd been overwhelmed, initially, by the array of charts, statistics, and theories those accountants had presented for his study.

Value represents for each of us that which we ourselves want in life. Simple enough, surely! If nobody wanted gold, the general disinterest would deprive gold of its value. A Van Gogh painting is valuable to the extent that people *give* it value. Their desire is what determines its price. If no one wanted it, it would be no more valuable than any piece of damaged canvas of comparable size.

Next to desirability as a criterion of wealth is the ease or difficulty we'd have in obtaining what we want. Air, for example, though a life necessity, is available everywhere; therefore we don't attach great value to it. Were it suddenly to become scarce, however, it would be worth up to everything we possess. Van Gogh's "Starry Night," on the other hand, is not even available in the original. Were it for sale, some people would desire it so greatly that its monetary value, for them, would be enormous.

If an object is desirable, but can be obtained only at the effort, let us say, of traversing vast deserts, scaling high mountains, and braving stormy seas, it would have far more value for us than if it could be bought at the local supermarket.

Total lack of availability would deprive it of its appeal. Many other things, besides, might lose their appeal if the trouble of obtaining them were too great. The important thing, in this case, is to keep your desires within the bounds of your capabilities. Those stormy seas, for instance, might appear simply too great an obstacle when added to the difficulty of crossing vast deserts and scaling high mountains. (A young swain comes to mind who wrote to his beloved saying that, for her, he'd willingly brave deserts, high mountains, and stormy seas. In a short postscript, he added, "I'll visit you next Saturday, if it isn't raining.")

Adam Smith wrote that the value of a thing is determined by the effort that went into its production. "Labour alone," he stated, "never varying in its own value, is alone the ultimate and real standard by which the value of all commodities can at all times and places be estimated and compared. It is their real price; money is their nominal price only." Earlier, we saw that Karl Marx offered the same criterion. What both of those men said is no doubt true when applied, as they intended, to factory workers. They themselves allowed for differences of skill and speed in one's work. As we pointed out earlier, however, the amount of time that goes into something complex like building a home is by no means the only criterion of its value. Finally it comes down to the care and intelligence that went into designing and constructing the home, not merely to the labor that went into building it. Other criteria are important also. "Demand"—the term economists use—depends also on such factors as appearance, design, location, and the neighborhood around the home. Value, from the point of view of demand, is entirely subjective. Some people would pay large sums of money for a pair of shoes worn by a famous golfer when winning a major championship. The trophy would be meaningless to anyone who had no interest in golf.

Money is wealth only to the extent that it can be used in exchange for the things one wants. It is useless to an Eskimo, for example, in the snowy wastes he inhabits, for nothing exists around him for sale. And it is useless to someone who doesn't want what can be exchanged for money.

Several years ago I went on vacation to a Latin American country. On my return to America, the customs officer glanced at my declaration on the form and exclaimed, "I can't believe it! Seventeen *cents!* Is that really *all* you spent?" We had a good laugh. I'd bought nothing that whole week but a pocket comb. What did it matter to me what the prices were, since I'd seen nothing there that I wanted?

Local manufacturers might have tried to whet my appetite with advertisements for their products. That is why advertisers are hired: both to tell people that the product exists and to give the product itself an aura of attractiveness. Advertising is a service to people if it informs them of an object's availability. It is arguably amoral, however, if its sole purpose is to inflame people's desire for it. Indeed, the desire for unnecessary "necessities" is the silken cord that binds modern civilization to the wheel of perennial dissatisfaction.

In Panama some years ago, the United Food Company was distressed because its women workers remained at their jobs only two months a year. During the other months they lived on their earnings. Then a bright lad in the company had an inspiration: Why not send every woman a Sears Roebuck catalogue? The catalogues were sent, and the problem ceased: The women returned to work, and remained there uncomplainingly the whole year around.

Adam Smith's analysis of value must be considered in the context of one of his purposes, which was to protect the factory worker from selfish employers who were interested only in boosting their profits, and therefore in keeping the wages as low as possible while they squeezed all the work out of their employee that they could. Given the circumstances, the quality of the work was probably, as Adam Smith said, fairly uniform. It would be a mistake, he argued, to value such work at no more than the cost of slave labor.

Karl Marx, on the other hand, cannot be so easily exonerated, for he placed supreme importance on labor itself, regardless of any thought and care that goes into designing and making a product. His system was a disaster for society, for it enforced conformity to a mindlessly controlled system, run by people as indifferent to the quality of the work as were the workers themselves. In Russia many years ago, a Western visitor was taken around a factory where he found what looked like evidence at last of real efficiency. It was a factory that made signs, and its products were stacked everywhere. He asked his guide, "What do those signs say?" Her answer was, "They say, 'Out of order.'"

It has been wisely said that a society is known by the people it considers great. The heroes of Marxist society are those men and women with the least commitment to anybody's welfare. Their service is to "the system." Some of those "heroes" butchered people by the thousands to achieve their envied status.

Adam Smith did at least try to uplift society materially, by emphasizing free enterprise. The "upliftment" Marx offered was an outright deception. He hailed as the nation's best citizens those who, in other societies, have usually attracted the least admiration. Such people were, he said, the true aristocrats. This appellation was merely theoretical. The power it implied was that of the mob.

Intelligent people are more and more coming to realize that wealth is not a *thing* so much as a manifestation of well-directed energy. It is not the result only of muscular labor, but of thought, of sensitive appreciation for beauty, of concern for usefulness, and, if you will, of love. If one were to lose everything materially, but still possess his creativity, he might justifiably claim to be richer than another who had inherited millions, but lacked the creativity to put his money to productive use. Wealth that is too easily acquired might even be placed in quotation marks, for it represents capital with little likelihood of further gain. In time, it will dwindle away. Interestingly in this context, I am told (whether rightly or not I don't know) that the Vanderbilt family, once mighty in the world of finance, has lost all its wealth.

Adam Smith's general thesis was that every human being is motivated primarily by self-interest. A nation's prosperity, he said, will soar if it gives people the freedom to improve their own lot. "It is not," he wrote, "from the benevolence of the butcher, the brewer, or the baker that we expect our dinner, but from their regard to their own interest. We address ourselves, not to their humanity, but to their self-love, and never talk to them of our own necessities, but of their advantages." Passages like this caused an outcry among *soi-disant* champions of morality, though in fact Smith had simply stated an obvious truth. He was comparing self-interest to false morality, which bases generosity and benevolence entirely on self-denial. Smith was right, of course. Morality, as people usually define it, is hypocrisy. No one will *really* help another if he expects only, in doing so, to become miserable. Self-sacrifice for others should be for the sake of a greater good. If it benefits oneself also, if only in terms of inner satisfaction, it is no sacrifice. Smith erred only, as many self-styled moralists have done, by not humanizing his subject enough. He didn't focus with sufficient clarity on the people's actual needs, as individuals.

He gave us examples—the butcher, the brewer, the baker—to support his argument. What he didn't do was give us human beings: He gave us two-dimensional tradesmen. It might have helped had he given those tradesmen names, personalities, families.

Let us make up for this "sin of omission." We'll name the baker, William—surname, Baker. And we'll assume the presence of another one in town, whom we'll name Joe—surname, Crumpet. Let us be even more specific. William concentrates only on the advantages accruing to himself while he sells bread, whereas Joe, though fully aware that he is earning a living, has other values besides. He greets you with a smile, treats you as a friend, asks after your family, hopes that you enjoy his baked goods, perhaps solicits your advice on how to improve them.

Let us now assume—it is probably the case anyway—that William wears a perennially grim expression, that he has poor digestion, and is always bitter about something. Joe, on the other hand, is warm-hearted, healthy, and happy. Isn't it likely that, quite apart from economic considerations—their products bear more or less the same prices—you'll shop at Joe's, and shun William as a bad omen?

Adam Smith, in discussing economics, discounted more human considerations such as benevolence because he considered these to lie outside the circle he'd drawn. He wanted to convince his readers that he, too, was a scientist. Whence, however, that word, *benevolence?* Whence other words like it, such as kindness, sympathy, compassion, and good will? These must have *some* meaning. If they haven't any for the economist, perhaps the fault lies in the way he approaches his science.

Let us imagine a final possibility: What if William—not Joe, mind you, for whom we have a natural liking, but William, for whom we have little—is stricken by tragedy? His home may have burned down, or his only child just died. Wouldn't you rush to bring him and his family comfort and assistance, offering them money, food, clothing, sympathy? Financial considerations wouldn't enter the picture. Even your personal feelings for him, which have been at best tepid, would pale to insignificance before his great loss.

Adam Smith, being an economist, ignored such considerations as irrelevant. Economic constructs, however, if kept apart from human realities, are no better than wax images. They may be artful, but they lack life. Being only wax, moreover, they melt under the heat of scrutiny and become shapeless. If there is any subject that affects our lives daily, it is just this one, economics, which Smith separated so carefully from the life we actually live. We ought to give highest economic consideration to human values: not as statistics, merely, but for their meaning to us as individuals. We ought to see people, too, in terms of the *awareness* they project. This is their primary reality, for us.

Smith was right in saying that every human being is motivated primarily by self-interest. What he missed, since he was concentrating on mechanisms, was the simple fact that self-interest is directional: leading inward toward greater self-absorption, or outward, toward greater self-expansion. In the first case, it shrinks a person's awareness inward upon himself. The result is slowly decreasing personal satisfaction and happiness. In the second case it expands one's consciousness. The result is ever-increasing personal contentment and fulfillment.

Self-interest need not be selfish. In itself, it is only self-awareness, which has a natural impulse toward expansion. In expansion it finds fulfillment. Contractiveness, on the contrary, which squeezes one's self-identity, brings him increasing frustration and disappointment.

True expansion of self-identity comes not with an increasing number of possessions, nor with power over greater numbers of people, but with growing sympathy and understanding. Such expansion means broadening one's identity with others, including their needs in one's own needs instead of trying to force everything and everybody into an orbit around one's own little ego.

This atom, the ego, is obliged of its own nature to view everything filtered through its self-awareness. This awareness begins small, like an atom drifting alone in space. If the atom happens to collide with another, their united gravity, though still tiny, increases. Gradually, other atoms join them, and their gravity field slowly increases, until finally great clouds of atoms are drawn to them even from millions of miles away.

Thus too, as the ego acquires experiences, develops its own attitudes, and acquires new characteristics, it develops a field of energy comparable to gravity—call it magnetism—attracting to itself increasing understanding, power, and sensitive awareness.

In the case of atoms, when they are united in sufficient numbers a star is born. Similarly, as people increase their awareness and intelligence, their "magnetism" (so called) increases until, like stars in the firmament of humanity, they radiate light to everyone they meet.

Sometimes in the vastness of space a star implodes, to become what is known in astronomy as a black hole, the density of which is so enormous that not even light escapes it. Egoic self-involvement, similarly—the opposite of expansive self-interest—is implosive. Its psychological density can become extreme. Pride and selfishness shrink a person's consciousness until, figuratively speaking, in his total self-absorption no radiance escapes him.

Such is the direction of development for the William Bakers of this world, though few of them ever become so psychologically imploded as to deserve comparison to black holes. The Joe Crumpets, on the other hand, radiate light outward to others. Like stars, their sympathies shine expansively. They enjoy sharing, and have no wish to draw possessively to themselves. Self-interest, for both the Crumpets and the Bakers, is a reality, but the Crumpets are wise enough to realize that fulfillment comes from sharing with others, not by absorbing their energy and happiness for their own gain.

Enlightened self-interest is far from contradicting traditional ethics. Indeed, it is the only true basis for ethics there is. Unenlightened self-interest, on the other hand, goes against human nature itself. In drawing happiness inward to itself it limits its horizons, finally to the point of self-suffocation.

In saying, "I appreciate other people's needs and interests, as I do my own; I appreciate their friendship; I appreciate the realities they share with me," one places himself in harmony with others and with nature's ways. Self-expansion is self-ennobling. Self-ennoblement, in return, is self-expansive. How different, this perception of nobility, from the conceptions of Adam Smith, Karl Marx, and Machiavelli! To Adam Smith, nobility meant wealth. To Marx, genuine aristocracy was a "dictatorship of the proletariat." To Machiavelli, nobility meant the power wielded by a ruler. But true nobility is dominion of another kind. It expands one's self-interest to a sense of identity with others. Originally, the term *aristocrat* was equated with nobility of character. It had little or nothing to do with property or monetary wealth.

In ancient India, the ruling class were the *kshatriya*s, or "warriors," a symbolic name which signified willingness to sacrifice their own lives for their countrymen. Over centuries this ideal was lost, to the point where aristocracy came to signify a merely hereditary privilege. Wealthy landowners and military leaders claimed the right to be served, and never thought in terms of serving others.

Social distinction in Western countries, though bestowed primarily on the wealthy, was sometimes given also to those who were well educated and who possessed at least a veneer of refinement. This was the sole remaining instance of a previously common perception that respect is due above all to those who deserve it personally. In truth, there have always been peasants who were nobler by nature than most so-called aristocrats. In other words, there has always been a true, as opposed to a false, conventional, nobility. True nobility is based on personal worth. False nobility is based on the "counterfeit" value of worldly power and a large bank account.

Democracy is an attempt to rectify aristocratic abuses by claiming that everyone is an aristocrat. Not many people deserve that high rank, of course, except in the latent potential everyone has in his humanity. To pretend that everyone is noble is to robe the veriest ditch-digger in a silk robe of imaginary majesty. Dull minds are fit only for manual labor; they express human potential in its lowest form. It is not from such people that one expects the creative spirit needed for progress. Dullards have very little sense of responsibility to others, and still less to society as a whole. For this reason alone, ditch-diggers and the like are not worthy of the encomiums lavished on them by Karl Marx. Demagogues assure people, especially those who don't care to think for themselves, "You're as good as the best!" And what is the result? As their sense of self-worth grows, bloated by flattery, true nobility is mocked at as artificial and no longer worth emulating; rather, people suspect it doesn't even exist. Thus, nobility is equated with mediocre intelligence and with "people power," and anyone even moderately thoughtful is denounced as a parasite.

I recall in the 1940s, as a delayed echo from the "thirties," how intellectuals would affect "earthy" language and attitudes to impress others with their own "basic realism." This was a pose, merely. In the 1950s, beatnik poets with masters degrees in literature would affect bad grammar so as not to be mistaken for dreamers whose heads were in the clouds. During the hippie movement of the 1960s and '70s, intellectuals adopted a whole new language to show that they were not "highfalutin'," parasitic, or unreal. Poses, all, in a sorry attempt to show that they were "as real, man," as your local ditch-digger, and capable of being quite as grubby as he after his hard day's work. Thank you, Karl Marx. You've given mankind a new goal to strive for: mindless, heedless, gut-centered stupidity, with the primal force of raw emotion that Tennessee Williams expressed with such grunting eloquence in his plays.

Unless this way of thinking is corrected, it will cause the downfall of democracy itself. For what will ensue, once the majority are invited to arbitrate everything including moral issues, is that emotions will come to dominate the public's consciousness. By emotions I mean the outraged denunciation of anything that doesn't meet with mass approval; loud acclamation for every passing fad; refusal to listen to any point of view different from one's own; and support for anything demanded by "the people." Wisdom itself becomes redefined to signify whatever reflects the "will of the people."

Elections determined by considerations such as these cannot fail, in time, to bring economic disintegration, as candidates realize there is no point in being over-scrupulous in the promises they make. "Everyone," they assure their electorate, "will have whatever he or she desires. You all *deserve* the best!" The ensuing "benefits" are, of course, funded by tax money, which in turn is filtered through the sieve of ever-expanding governmental control. In the process, the costs add up. And whence comes all that money? Initially—one suspects—from many who never voted for those "representatives" in the first place.

When the need for tax money exceeds people's willingness to be taxed, a solution is ready to hand: Increase the money supply! Monetary inflation destroys, ultimately, the value of money itself. This is called "hidden taxation."

What occurs is that government-guaranteed security becomes the general goal, in time. People prefer it to personal integrity. The government, in trying to give people everything they want, robs them of their freedoms. For the larger a government is, and the greater the people's sense of security under its protection, the more their liberty is lost altogether.

The larger a government, moreover, the less the prosperity a nation creates. For bureaucrats, generally speaking, are not competent businessmen. People with business skills are attracted to the private sector, where creativity is prized.

An example of the business ineptitude of governments is evident in the U.S. Post Office. Many years ago, first-class postage stamps cost only three cents. Today, they cost thirty-four. The ostensible goal of this large price increase—80%, adjusted for inflation—is improved efficiency. Accompanying the rise in the cost of stamps, however, has been an actual *decline* in efficiency.

Many years ago I wrote to the U.S. Post Office in Washington D.C. to complain of the glue they were using on their air letter forms. "I lick the flap," I said, "but it won't seal. The moment the paper dries, it comes unstuck." Now, commercial envelopes, available in stationery stores and markets everywhere, have never posed this problem. Couldn't the government have learned this elementary lesson from private industry? The reply I received told me that this idea hadn't occurred to them. "We are aware of the problem you mention," the letter assured me, "and are experimenting with different glues. We confidently expect to have the matter resolved before long." Has the problem ever been solved? I don't know. Nowadays, I use e-mail.

I don't think an exhaustive study of various types of government, and of possible solutions to the problems connected with creeping bureaucracy, would accomplish anything positive. I suspect the problem can't be solved, at least not given present realities.

Democracy was established because people had grown fed up with oligarchy (rule by a few) and wanted freedom. Freedom, however, cannot survive if people decide they'd rather be secure. Democracy, in this case, eventually becomes replaced again by oligarchy, and the cycle continues indefinitely.

Human nature being what it is, it is doubtful whether any system will provide a permanent solution. Systems can't ensure anything that isn't backed by the will of the people. The best system imaginable cannot but fail, if those living under it are not interested in making it work. And the worst system will somehow totter along if its citizens have that will. It isn't that good systems aren't worthwhile, but only that they are accompanied by no guarantees.

Consider Adam Smith's argument for free enterprise. Yes, it *ought* to work. No controlled economy, certainly, has ever shown, or ever could show, itself capable of producing wealth. Free enterprise, in which everyone is at liberty to promote his own well-being, is the only system so far that shows any promise. Does this mean it is perfect? Far from it!

The greatest problem with free enterprise is that large, wealthy, powerful companies are able to use their power to suppress competition. Let us say someone creates a new product, and forms a company to manufacture and sell it. What happens next? An already-established, already-wealthy, already-powerful corporation produces a similar product, and sells it at a loss with the sole intention of driving the "little guy" out of business. What is the poor fellow to do?

People nowadays run to "Big Daddy," or "Big Brother"—in other words, they seek government intervention, urging Congress to pass a law that will make unfair practices like this impossible. At first, government interference looks good. It is only a stopgap measure, however. Government interference grows, as similar issues arise. Its largeness fans the legislators' sense of self-importance, which in turn develops in them a certain feeling of kinship with bigness everywhere. Big government, by the very nature of things, ends up favoring big corporations, even though its original *raison d'être* was concern for the "little guy." Meanwhile, things reach a point, eventually, where new companies can barely open their doors to do business after they've complied with all the fussy regulations. For when they've finally satisfied those official requirements, they find they have little left actually to run their business!

Are there possible alternatives? Here's a suggestion: Instead of running to "Big Daddy" for help, why not diversify what you sell? If competition undercuts a single product, the business may survive long enough on other resources for its competitors to tire of the game, and let the little fellow have his profits after all.

Whether any specific "little guy" finds this suggestion feasible, it may at least inspire him to try to develop "solution-consciousness," and to study the possibilities for other answers. In time he may find that there are many feasible alternatives. Every viable alternative will re-emphasize the worth, incentive, and capabilities of the individual. A spirit of self-reliance will automatically discourage the practice—almost a conditioned reflex by now—of running to "Big Daddy" for help. Here, in fact, we arrive at a new concept of wealth, one very different from what Adam Smith proposed in *The Wealth of Nations.*

What *is* wealth, really? A person has it in proportion to what he possesses that he himself values. He is *not* wealthy in proportion merely to other people's envy of him, except perhaps to the extent that he values that envy and the shallow importance he imagines it gives him.

Wealth should not be considered in terms of what other people find desirable. It should be defined in terms of one's own desires, and one's own values. Having established these values, a person should live by them faithfully.

Food, clothing, shelter: These are universal needs. If a person has them, and desires nothing more, he is already wealthy. Beyond that, the struggle for wealth is arduous and never-ending. To a great extent, it is a useless quest for non-essentials, and leaves one maimed in spirit if not in limb; weary, disillusioned, and increasingly unhappy. And what lesson is learned from it at last? that it has all been for nothing! Everything, in the end, must be abandoned.

People's concept of wealth is focused far too narrowly on what others think of them, from a desire for their envy. When that envy is desired, what one really wants is others' unhappiness compared to his own. How can so ignoble a desire fail to create enemies? The more enemies one has, the more one feels the need to protect himself, to be forever wary and fearful.

Appreciation for the happiness of others, on the

other hand, wins their friendly appreciation in return. It makes friends of them. A person surrounded by friends is relaxed in the knowledge that they will support him in his need. As his identity expands beyond the narrow confines of selfhood and self-preoccupation, he finds happiness in himself. Self-interest is self-fulfilling if it is directed outward to embrace others as part of one's own reality. When self-interest contracts inward, however, separating itself from others and from life, it produces, as we have seen, inner suffering. The worst disease of modern times is a surfeit of the wrong kind of wealth: attachment to an ever-increasing number of possessions. These become obsessions, eventually to possess us in return.

Life, for most people, is a treadmill. There is no end to the weary trudge so long as one's desires are centered in dreams of self-aggrandizement. If there is a better way, it can be found not in grandiose schemes for world betterment, but in a search for personal fulfillment. Once the right way to this fulfillment is found, its benefits become obvious. The lesson will spread naturally, by example. Those grandiose schemes for social betterment are like splashes of rose water onto a muddy pond: The fragrance is nullified immediately by the stench of ambition and selfish desires. The way to true fulfillment lies in expanding, not in contracting, one's sympathies. A person should expand his interest in life and his concern for others until he is able to declare, "Self-interest, rightly understood, is the essence of true wisdom."

If you decide to change your life's patterns, and if experience shows you that this has been a good decision, others will be inspired to change themselves as you did. The change—yours, and then theirs—must be voluntary. It must not be embraced for the vague sake of "humanity," nor to please anyone else. Indeed, it would be a mistake to think that because any specific idea is good it must therefore be universally adopted. One system for all may be feasible for colonies of ants, but it won't work for human beings. Humanity is too complex for any one person, or even a few people, to solve all its problems. Do your best, instead, to shine in the little space you've been allotted. Inspire others also, as you are able, to develop their own light. But don't presume to tell anyone *how* to shine. And don't expect anyone merely to reflect your own light. The best thing you can do for "humanity" is to *encourage* a few others toward their own self-development.

Be noble in the true sense, then! To own land will not make you so. Riches won't do it. People's envy will not enhance your real worth. Seek wealth in faithfulness to your own ideals. Be true, first of all, to your own happiness. Why honor other people's definition of wealth? Why follow the flock, while the sheep dog, public opinion, barks at your heels to keep you in line?

The best posture to assume is to stand on your own two feet! And what is the best attitude? To turn to new advantage the common question, "What's in it for me?" by asking, "What will truly promote my own happiness?" Meanwhile, what is all that barking about? Isn't the sheep dog only telling you, "Don't look for happiness! Be like everyone else. See what fun they're having, snatching and grabbing everything they can from one another!"

Community is a basic human need. The question when seeking it should be, "With whom shall I mix?" Crucial to the answer is another question: "Why these people, particularly?" Most people see no urgency in this last question. Yet they ought to. Usually, the "where, who, and why" of community is determined by such superficial considerations as nearness to one's work, social prestige, schooling for the children, and shopping convenience. Yet people, too, are important to us—for themselves, and for the influence they have on our lives.

From birth onward we are thrust among other people. We depend on them for our strength, knowledge, emotional support, experience, and wisdom. And we need, for our own mental, moral, and spiritual development, to be able to offer them support in return. Such, realistically speaking, is the Social Contract, toward which the philosophers Hobbes, Locke, and Rousseau were reaching. They, however, thought in terms of people's relationship to their governments, not of their responsibility to themselves and to one another. A tacit admission of interdependence exists between all members of a society. It is the true benefit of civilization.

Why continue plodding numbly down the same worn lane, once you've seen that life is not giving you what you hoped for? Why not seek companions from whom you might gain greater satisfaction than the mere convenience of having company? Indeed, why not seek others for their compatibility with your own higher aspirations?

People do not necessarily achieve wisdom with age. Often, all they achieve is girth and increased foolishness. Whole societies sometimes err in basic ways. A person who wants to improve his life meaningfully must struggle uphill to realize that desire, against countless descending influences. Why not augment your strength by associating with people who share your goals in life?

One reason people need one another is that they dread the yawning emptiness in themselves. They are lonely, and depend, consequently, on outer stimulation. Strange to say, they fear even to be inspired, lest inspiration force them to think deeply! They seek community with others as a way of escape.

Sooner or later, however, they will have to face the ultimate reality: their own selves. Why waste a whole lifetime? Why not seek out friends in whose company you can find challenge and upliftment?—companions who can reinforce the potential you know exists in yourself. Only such people can be your true friends. Others are mere "fillers"!

Think, finally, what it would mean to bring unity to your life. Job, friends, home, church, school, recreation: all in one place. This is what a well-formed community would offer. Instead of scattering the energy you devote to these pursuits, bring a clear focus to your life. Modern life, lacking this focus, has become fragmented. Bestowing no inner peace, it creates a spirit of restlessness and deep unhappiness.

Small communities, in which people live together for their own and for one another's true fulfillment, are surely a goal worth striving toward for everyone anxious to find a solution to life's problems.

CHAPTER SEVEN

Communities and Social Responsibility

Part of what might, tongue in cheek, be called the "American mystique" is the lone cowboy—movies with Gary Cooper spring to mind—riding into town with easy nonchalance, indifferent to the hostility and fear all around him.

I saw an interesting example of this attitude during a television interview many years ago. The guest was one of those laconic, "do your own thing" people. He *was,* however, a guest, and had accepted the invitation of his own free will. He had, therefore, at least *some* of the obligations of that role. The host, intrigued by the man's aloofness, managed nevertheless to treat him courteously.

Halfway through the interview, the visitor stood up from his seat, draped his jacket nonchalantly over one shoulder, and left the room without a backward glance. The camera followed him all the way to the door. This indifference to the opinion of others has lingered in my mind as a statement of individuality that seemed very American, impressive in its own way, but insulting also, and insensitive. Was this behavior an example of Emersonian "self-reliance"? Was it a demonstration of personal integrity? It struck me, rather, as a deliberate pose behind which pride hid its sneering face.

So far in this book, I have emphasized the need for individual integrity, the need to be motivated from within rather than by crowds, and the need to develop self-understanding before trying to understand other people. It is, however, important to recognize the difference between integrity and arrogance. One may remove himself aloofly from others in the false belief that he has nothing in common with them. In fact, however, all human beings, in the simple fact of their humanity, are inherently the same. However distinct in appearance, all of them are parts of one whole.

One of the main objections people make to anyone who goes off to do something different is that it shows an absence of social responsibility. Their first objection is merely to the novelty of his act. We've heard the saying, "They laughed at Fulton." Robert Fulton invented a ship made of metal, and his detractors laughed because, as everyone knows, metal is heavier than water. "Common sense" told them the ship would sink. People also scoffed at the heavier-than-air flying machine built by Orville and Wilbur Wright. In this case again, success silenced the critics. Today's "folk wisdom" declares, "All attempts so far to create intentional communities have failed." Perhaps, after one or even several new communities have proved successful, the critics will again be silenced. In time, the comment everywhere may be, "But of course! I'm thinking of living in such a community myself." Meanwhile, the important thing is not to *deserve* the wet sponge. In other words, do as Robert Fulton did, as the Wright brothers did: Rely on practical, not on theoretical, common sense, based on reasoned thought and on frank openness to trial and error. Don't be vague in your idealism, as many have been in the past, in the delusion that a quasi-visionary spirit put them in automatic contact with higher realities.

Beyond viewing newness as merely bizarre, many people are inclined to consider anyone who chooses a different road to be eccentric, socially irresponsible, and perhaps even anti-social. Why so? Numerous experiments are needed nowadays, if society is to develop further and not stagnate in a pond of scum-formed traditions. Would it be anti-social in a lemming to hold back, while the others plunged off a cliff to their watery grave? It is wise, sometimes, to step back a little from the stampede of opinion and re-think one's priorities. The need for greater clarity has become urgent in this age, for there have been unsettling developments in people's perceptions of reality. Scientific discoveries threaten to overwhelm the common trust in human values. Before such rapidly expanding vistas of reality it is difficult to make moral adjustments.

We are accustomed to consider alternatives as a choice between opposites: the "either/or" options of Aristotelian logic. Georg Hegel, the German philosopher, refined this mode of reasoning to its ultimate degree with his statement, "All that is real is rational, and all that is rational is real." Hegel developed what he termed the "dialectical" method for arriving at truths: *thesis, antithesis,* and *synthesis.* Two opposites (thesis and antithesis), when contrasted, produce a synthesis. This synthesis, according to him, is a new truth. His philosophy left no room for subtler-than-rational inspirations.

Hegel was committed to establishing a spiritual absolute, something he tried to hem in by rationality. He may have derived his dialectic from the ancient Indian concept of *dwaita* (duality), considering that the Indian scriptures were already beginning in his day to appear in European translations. In the Indian teachings, the cosmos consists of vibrations. These vibrations, at the end of manifested creation, subside into the oneness of absolute spirit. If indeed Hegel developed his system on the basis of those writings, it must be added that he botched the job. For the concept of *dwaita* implies— indeed necessitates—movement. The Indian absolute is not a "synthesis" of that movement, but is simply the cessation of movement altogether.

Hegel's "thesis" and "antithesis," being rational concepts, are—unlike the vibrations of *dwaita*—fixed and unmoving. His "synthesis," too, suggests merely a resolution of two antithetical positions into a new one, equally fixed.

The example is often given, in order to explain Hegel, of the birth of America. First, there was eighteenth-century England (thesis); then the American Revolution (antithesis); and finally the appearance of the new American nation (synthesis). This comparison is hardly convincing. America after the Revolution represented, in many ways, no mere reaction to England and its governmental system: It was an entirely new development. George Washington, Thomas Jefferson, and John Adams—these men particularly, the three main architects of the new nation—were learned scholars, extensive readers, and deep thinkers. They incorporated into their political schema a prolonged study of ancient philosophies and civilizations. What they developed, moreover, was no mere synthesis of other people's ideas. Certainly it was not limited to the differences between England and America. The inspiration of those men, indeed, drew from many streams of thought—from, if you will, many "theses" and "antitheses." At this point, however, Hegel's whole dialectic breaks down, for many of those ideational streams were in no way antithetical to one another, but mutually supportive. What emerged in the minds of those early Americans was not a synthesis: It was something vital, and not anticipated in any of those ancient writings.

Marx, Engels, and Lenin, unfortunately, found Hegel's rational dialectic attractive, and used it for the basis of their own philosophy—"purged," as Karl Marx put it, of its mystifying preoccupation with "absolutes." Hegel's thinking permitted ongoing creativity, but Marx and his fellow communists, having "cleansed" the system, as they claimed, gave it the new name, "dialectical materialism." In their minds, the application of Hegelian "synthesis" to communism resolved the struggle between capital and the proletariat, and brought the evolution of social history to a full stop in their vision of communism, society's "glorious and ineluctable destiny." Communists today, armed with their pretentious "dialectical materialism," scoff at ideas that are not in keeping with their own concept of reality. Such a fantasy of wishful thinking would put even lemmings to shame, if they gave such matters a thought!

Soviet writers—so we are told by Lewis S. Feuer*—"have derided the genetics of Gregor Mendel, the finite universe of Albert Einstein, the physical principle of indeterminacy, and Sigmund Freud's psychoanalysis as 'idealistic' and 'undialectical.'"

---

*Professor of Philosophy, University of Vermont, quoted in *Encyclopedia Americana*, Vol. 8, p. 59 (1967).

It is precisely this suggestion of rational finalities that constitutes the great weakness in Hegel's dialectic. How can a rational synthesis become, in its turn, a springboard for further invention? The very purpose of "synthesis," like a compromise between arguing factions in parliament, is to halt further debate.

It may be helpful, in fact, to consider a different concept from Hegel's altogether: not "dialectical," but *discursive.* I give it this name because it invites ongoing, and even friendly, dialogue. The terms I propose for discursive reasoning are the following: *action, reaction,* and *interaction.*

Hegel's dialectic, when contrasted with discursiveness, offers definitions that are rigidly fixed. In normal life, however, it isn't so much our definitions as our behavior that determines the right or wrong of a thing. What, we ask ourselves, is the result of a course of action? Drunkenness may seem pleasurable for a time—to the drinker—but if he indulges in it too frequently he may bring himself to personal ruin. Drunkenness in any case is not a thesis: It is a direction of energy, of movement. Interaction, then, suggests back and forth movement—like the ripples on a pond into which some heavy object has been dropped. Moving outward in all directions, the ripples hit the bank, return, then crisscross back and forth repeatedly. In that interacting motion there is no finality—unless it be an eventual cessation of movement. Instead, there is a possibility of the formation of continually interesting patterns. In human interaction, similarly, there is a possibility of continuous communication, of ever-fresh discoveries arising from sources that may even be unrelated, rather than a simple synthesis between antithetical ideas.

To Hegel's way of thinking, any new proposal rates as an "antithesis" to old concepts, suggesting conflict rather than harmonious development. To do anything new and different is, according to his view, to set oneself *against* what is being done already. Why should this be so? If one thinks in terms of action and reaction, instead of thesis and antithesis, and if the result is *interaction,* one sees also the possibility for cooperation, rather than conflict. A new concept, in other words, need not *exclude* previous concepts. Small new communities, in this context, need in no way be considered antithetical to the society we know already. They may simply represent, and much more realistically, fresh patterns of social interaction.

In this view, personal integrity need in no way represent polarization of one group against another, or of new groups against established ones. It needn't be like the contempt displayed by that "do-your-own-thing" guest I watched on television years ago. Indeed, such flaunted "integrity" will have only limited effectiveness, if any, in its assumption of a combative stance.

We all belong to one race: humanity. To try to

function outside that parameter is not only unrealistic, but a foolish waste of energy.

Years ago in India, I visited a community that boasted the intention of becoming fully self-sufficient. Visitors were shown, prominently displayed on a board, a water faucet that had been cast in the community's own foundry. I couldn't help smiling to myself. What was the point, I thought, of making a faucet that could be purchased for a fraction of the cost at any hardware store? That the community should aspire to be self-sustaining was reasonable. But to aspire to become in this way completely self-sufficient would be sensible only if the members found themselves stranded, like the Swiss Family Robinson, on some desert island. (And even those doughty pioneers had access to many modern products, which they rescued from the wreckage of their ship.)

In another community I visited, the group's whole energy was directed toward self-sufficiency through business. Could such an intense focus on profit, I wondered, justify their existence in the first place as a community? Their true purpose wasn't profit: It was independence. No doubt it was praiseworthy on their part to want financial independence, but if they had to define that independence in terms of mere profit, something infinitely more precious was in danger of being lost. The community's leaders, unlike its founder, were businessmen at heart. Yet the most saleable "item" they had to offer was the very concept of independence. Could not promoting that concept have become also a source of income for them? Otherwise, what inspiration could be found in merely producing shoes for profit—strictly for profit? (This, in fact, *was* their business.)

The communitarian concept proposed in this book is dynamic. It is by no means a static process of "thesis" and "antithesis" resulting in "synthesis." It offers alternatives to a vast number of modern ills: to society's emphasis on unnecessary consumerism; to diffused rather than focused human energy; to the frenzy of "keeping up with the Joneses"; and to the rudeness one encounters so often in big-city life. On the other hand, it also offers an alternative to the traditional small village, where petty gossip, a shallow outlook, lack of contact with the outside world, and lack of charity toward one another tend to dull people's minds.

My father worked for several years in New York City—the epitome, nowadays, of the Big City. He told us he'd once asked a subway attendant whether such-and-such a train went to Long Island. The man looked him up and down briefly, sneered, then demanded, "You can *read,* can't ya?" That having been said, he turned away indifferently without further reply.

People who praise social responsibility usually mean nothing more than a lemming-like plunge into the ocean of big-city life. A line from a poem I wrote while I lived outside New York City with my parents stated, "Men never more than glance at things for fear of missing one." This, to me, describes, even more so today than it did then, what passes for "life" in modern times. It is America. It is the big city. It is New York. It is also Anywhere that people live and struggle in too-close proximity to one another.

Several years ago, in a barbershop in Rome, Italy, I was subjected to the distraction of a television set chattering away to "entertain" the customers—or, perhaps, to entertain the barber himself. No scene, I noticed, was held longer than two seconds. Why, I thought, would anyone want to submit himself to this barrage of ceaseless restlessness?

Does it show concern for others merely to jostle and be jostled in return? I remember getting off the train from the suburbs at Grand Central Station in New York in those days, and telling myself firmly, "Today, I'm going to walk slowly." It was impossible. From the moment I emerged onto the street I found myself swept along by the "madding crowd." Had I sauntered as I'd intended, I'd have been bowled over from behind or from the side. Some people may find exhilaration in those hustling throngs. I never have.

Would a person be abdicating his social responsibilities if he shook the dust of such scenes off his feet? Would he be wrong in trying to do something else? If so, why? What does it add to anything to "fling roses, roses riotously with the throng" as the poet Ernest Dowson put it? Oh, I know: The "correct" answer is, It isn't the rushing; it's participating in modern life's great mechanism of commerce: Everyone's shoulder to the wheel; everyone working for the common goal: prosperity.

Again I ask: *Why?*

Frankly, I don't find the supposedly correct argument convincing. I see the modern drive for prosperity as a stampede. It is a disease: this compulsion to produce more and constantly more, but quite unnecessary, "necessities." Does it show a sense of responsibility to plunder our planet merely to satisfy humanity's insatiable greed? Does it show responsibility to keep feeding people's mounting dissatisfaction? Is this the way to husband the legacy Nature has so generously bestowed upon us? I see no altruism in this feeding frenzy. Rather, I see only Adam Smith's principle of self-interest being warped to its ultimate and worst consequences: selfishness, not self-expansion. To pretend otherwise is humbug. If one really had his heart set on being socially responsible, he would proceed serenely on his path through life instead of huffing and puffing to inflate the balloon of greed until it bursts from excessive debt.

Why "jive" with the gnats on a sunbeam? "Well," some may protest, "there are always the poor. If you really want to be serviceful, why not go serve in a soup kitchen?" This, certainly, would show some degree of responsibility, but is it the best way of helping others? And is it the only way? To help people learn to walk whose legs have been paralyzed, that a few of them may recover sufficiently to return to a so-called "normal" life of rushing headlong with the frenzied crowd? There seems something altogether wrong with this picture!

How many people get sucked into the social whirlpool not because they want to join in the "fun," but simply because they've never given the matter serious thought. They hurry anxiously down bustling streets, commute anxiously to work in stop-and-go traffic, anxiously collect their weekly paycheck, struggle anxiously through crowded traffic to get home—to what? Bills, debts, worry over what the neighbors think, and tension in the family. And after that—again: what? Someday, perhaps—so people tell themselves—they'll find happiness. What do they suppose happiness is? Is it a mere thing? Everything holds a mirror before us. Nothing will make us happy if we are not happy already in ourselves! Self-styled moralists will protest, "But, you're helping the economy!" Is that the "deeper" reason people go to Las Vegas and gamble?

"This above all," Polonius told Laertes in *Hamlet,* "to thine own self be true, and it shall follow as the night the day, thou canst not then be false to any man." Those words are often quoted, but, alas! rarely lived. If "charity begins at home"

(another oft-quoted saying), does not social responsibility begin there also? If, for example, I have no
inner peace, what peace will I share with anyone
else? Joining "peace marches" won't do it: colorful
placards and angrily shouted slogans. *Some* peace, I
must say! And if I have no self-understanding, is it
not presumptuous of me to pretend to understand
others? Life rushes on, and what awaits us at the
finish line? Death. And then what: oblivion?

We think to increase our understanding by
amassing more and more information, until our
brains are fairly bursting. For most people, life is a
cocktail party where one hurries from person to
person, from group to group, enthusing with
affected eagerness, "Hi, Joe! Oh, hiya, Jane!" only
hoping that he's got the names right.

Understanding of others comes with self-understanding. Since, however, even self-understanding
requires some human interaction, it is better to
interact with others in a meaningful way than
superficially. At a cocktail party, it would be better
to stop and talk a little with Joe or with Jane; to
become a little serious in your conversation with
them; to ask what they think about things both of
you consider important. Communication requires
more than foolish chatter: It requires calm feeling,
even intuition, to be true communication. Not emotion, mind you: The waves of emotional reaction
only distort clarity.

For such communication, people need time also

to be alone. Why do most cars on modern freeways carry only the driver? Highway planners keep trying to persuade people to travel in groups as a way of reducing congestion and gasoline consumption. They even reserve fast lanes for cars with more than one person. Still, the preference is for traveling alone. Why? The answer has to be that the ride to and from work is the only time people get away from all the noise at work, the noise at home, the noise on busy streets, the noise in crowded restaurants. It gives them a chance, perhaps, to listen to good recorded music, or to instructive recordings of talks. (Even so, how many people, out of sheer force of habit, switch their radios to excitedly babbling voices, or to the nerve-jangling beat of "music" from which the very plants have been found to recoil!)

People sometimes declare, "To love people, you've got to be *with* them!" Does running in a race make one more loving toward his competitors? To be with them calmly, however, not competitively: This is something the modern business atmosphere provides its workers all too little.

I noticed when traveling in India years ago that the cloth merchants in a small town had their shops in the same section. One would think that having all those shops selling the same products in close proximity to one another would be counterproductive. The system seemed to work for them, however. I observed no spirit of competition, no hostility between merchants. They appeared relaxed in the sales they were making. The system worked for them—first, it seemed to me, because everyone in town knew where to go for cloth; and second, because though buyers moved from shop to shop, the merchants evidently viewed one another rather in the light of colleagues than of competitors. Perhaps the fact of working side by side all their adult lives lessened the temptation for them to belittle one another's goods: They couldn't afford to endanger enduring relationships for the sake of merely momentary bargains. Indeed, I got the impression that many of them were friends. (After all, why shouldn't they be? They worked in the same line of business, and perhaps even lived in the same neighborhood.)

What made their relaxed attitude possible was that they saw no point in "thinking big." They made their profits, but beyond that maybe they thought it would poison their peace of mind to vie with one another for greater profit, especially if it might mean putting a colleague out of business. I'm perfectly certain that if some hustling American were to approach them with breathless advice on how to "win, win, win!" they'd consider him quite mad. Their values were human, not merely mercenary.

Let us consider again William Baker and Joe Crumpet, our two friends from the last chapter. Both men are bakers. Both men naturally want people to shop with them. If competition between them were to make them enemies, one of them might drive the other out of business. In this case, Joe Crumpet would probably be the winner. But would he still be smiling? Would he still be friendly to his customers? Wouldn't he be aware, rather, of Baker's bitterness directed now at him? And wouldn't he be uneasy in this knowledge? What is money, if its price is one's own peace of mind and the loss of all finer feelings?

What if Baker and Crumpet were to view each other, instead, as colleagues? What if they even kept shop next door to one another? Would not Baker be more inclined, at least, to *try* to be cheerful—if only because he'd notice that Crumpet's good cheer was drawing customers? Perhaps Crumpet, for his part, would discover some secret reason for Baker's gloom, and would try sympathetically to help him lighten his outlook. Perhaps both their businesses would thrive as a result of the friendly atmosphere surrounding their area of work.

In a small intentional community, where people who live together are bound by shared ideals, is it not far more likely that an easy spirit of cooperation will develop, as opposed to one of bitter competition? There is no reason why they shouldn't grow increasingly conscious that life has much more to offer than the usual so-called "bottom line": financial profit. Rather, a new "bottom line" may develop, one in which higher values are accepted as essential to true success. For success is far more than a bloated income, an impressive stock portfolio, and a bursting bank balance. Far more than these, success means friendship, peace of mind, happiness. There is no reason that others outside the community won't become friendly, too, at least in dealing with community members. For to give friendship is to attract it in return.

"Social responsibility" is a concept to furrow the brow. Grimly, the "responsible" citizen sets out to "do his duty by his fellowman." He may worry, in addition, about the starving Chinese. He may sigh for the people who died during an earthquake in Japan. He *cares,* you see. Indeed, it is good to care, though it is better to care usefully.

When I was a child, I often wouldn't finish my meals. My mother pleaded, "Think of all the starving people in China." In reply I would urge her, "Then please send them what I can't eat!" Compassion is far greater than pity. Obviously it is good to be compassionate, but one is more likely to be so if one is inwardly serene than if he bears the burden of worry about the "starving Chinese" in addition to his concerns over how to make ends meet, and how to pay this month's bills after all those purchases he placed on his credit cards.

Self-interest will no doubt be as much a factor in small-community life as it is in cities everywhere. In the communities I'm describing, however, the natural tendency will be not to enclose what one has, as if protectively, but rather to open the gates and greet everyone in the spirit that prevails among friends. Being surrounded by friends, rather than by mere neighbors, inclines one to see even the stranger as a friend, potentially.

What, by contrast, is the usual "community" spirit of modern city life? Here is a true story:

A couple, after living two years in an apartment, were on the point of moving out of it. Their suitcases were sitting on the mat outside their front door. A couple from an upstairs apartment, seeing their bags there, exclaimed, "You've just arrived! We want to welcome you. You'll find that we're all one big, happy family in this building. Do visit us any time you like." There followed the usual cocktail party smiles, and then it was off to other contacts—all of them, one suspects, as superficial as this one had been.

The poet John Donne declared in a well-known verse: "No man is an island." The sentiment is unambiguous, though if one reads it literally one may puzzle a bit. For if man isn't an island, what is he? a peninsula? a continent? a country surrounded by other countries? No island, moreover, is really isolated, for beneath the water's surface it protrudes, as we know, from the same earth which gives rise to every other land mass. No man is isolated from other members of the human race. In this perception, Donne stated a great truth. For all of us are part of the great network of life. The very atoms of our bodies have resided in countless other bodies—perhaps even, astronomers have postulated, in former universes.

The self-interest that Adam Smith promoted as the human norm is a contradiction to life's natural impulse. Self-interest of that kind contracts inward upon the ego, making one increasingly insular both in thought and in feeling. True wealth is whatever brings one true happiness. Even to promote the well-being of others, one's own first duty is to his own. Happiness can spread from one contented individual to many, but it can never spread from someone who merely trudges along on life's treadmill, determined to add his hard-earned mite to the Gross National Product. The best thing anyone can do for society is to focus on improving his own life, and—to whatever degree he is successful—to help others to improve their lives also. As far as specific contributions to the general well-being are concerned, the best one can bring to life's banquet table is one's own favorite dish. A farmer can grow the best food he can grow. A painter can contribute the best paintings he can execute. If the painter, accepting the advice of others, leaves off painting and becomes a banker, he may prove a failure.

We owe according to the kind and quantity of debts we've incurred. Obviously, we do have a certain debt to society. We owe it for the education we've received; for the language we speak and for the opportunity to express ourselves intelligibly; for the opportunity to be gainfully employed; for the quality of food and shelter available to us; for the fact that we have clothes to wear; for our very taste in clothing; and for many of our ideas on countless subjects. To repay those debts with lifelong servitude, however, would be to return misery in exchange for happiness! This would be no just recompense, surely. That we've received an education doesn't mean all of us must, out of gratitude, become school teachers. That we've learned to express ourselves intelligibly doesn't mean we should all become writers or orators. That we can be gainfully employed doesn't mean we should accept gainful employment at just any kind of job. That good food is available in the market doesn't mean we should help to produce it. Nor should we become builders, in gratitude for the fact that we live in houses. We owe something to the good taste of others, though I'm by no means certain that being stylish guarantees one's good taste.

Each of us has some special gift to offer to the world in return for what it has given us. It may be manual labor, or it may be artistic skill: no matter. If we take Adam Smith's dictum seriously, then self-interest is not only what we seek for ourselves, but what we enjoy doing and find fulfillment in doing.

Vincent Van Gogh is said to have earned the equivalent of only fifteen dollars from his paintings during his lifetime. His prosperous contemporaries must have thought him an utter failure. But what did those stolid burghers leave to the world compared to the joy he has brought to millions through his art? He lived to see little enough of people's appreciation, but there must have been joy in his own heart, considering he was able to produce an art that, since then, has given joy to so many people.

Nature doesn't ask us to give back *in kind*. We must give back *in spirit* what we've received. We must give because, in our own fulfillment, we fulfill life's plan for us, and for mankind. Our gratitude should be impersonal: not so much to Tim Wilson, who taught us mathematics at school, but to learning itself, and to wisdom.

Self-interest has many ramifications. We are taught to view it in terms of personal gain, but in the last chapter we saw that it includes all kinds of fulfillment, not the least of which is sharing our own happiness with others. Self-interest can also mean whatever each of us finds personally interesting. Our debt to society is best paid in terms of the *interest* we ourselves take in what we do. To do a thing well, we also must bring to it a high focus of energy. This we can do only if we love what it is we are doing.

Don't let anyone tell you what you *must* do. And don't expect to find perfection anywhere, or in any mere thing. People, after all, remain simply people. Gossip may still be a problem even in the most ideal community, though in the communities I'm describing gossip is usually an expression of concern for others rather than malicious prying. The antipathies and hurt feelings that sometimes arise between neighbors in a community are likely to diminish in force, at least, and may soon be dissipated. For when people live in close proximity to one another for idealistic reasons, and not only for economic advantage, they are inclined to soften their own hurts and antipathies by telling themselves, "Maybe I'm the one at fault. And if not, maybe there's something I can do anyway, to help matters."

Most suffering comes from holding false expectations. If we don't expect utopia, perhaps a little reflection will convince us that what we can gain by living in a community of true friends is far and away better than anything we ever had while stampeding with the herd.

CHAPTER EIGHT

❋

Darwinian Evolution and Consciousness

Every book I can remember reading on the subject of intentional communities—and I've read quite a few—seems to place its main emphasis on the system of government. For a long time those books convinced me that communities depend primarily on the way they are organized.

Life provided me also with experience in working with groups. At one time, I was responsible for developing centers to uphold certain principles. These centers were in several countries, and thus had diverse national attitudes. I hoped to create common guidelines that would be acceptable to all of them.

Eventually I had to yield to reality. Hegel's dictum, "All that is real is rational, and all that is rational is real," could never be applied to human beings—real enough in themselves, but by no means always rational! What I learned finally, against my own expectations, was that the spirit of a group depends *always* on one person. No system, however well conceived, can take the place of that person. Usually he, or she, is the leader, though not always so. He may be influential in other ways. Nevertheless, that person's presence in the group is more essential to it than any rule.

What convinced me at last of the need for a good leader was when the head of one of our best groups had, for reasons of health, to resign her position and withdraw from active participation. Soon thereafter, the others lost the vitality they'd shown as a unit, no longer displaying the same enthusiasm for working cooperatively.

Experience has convinced me, moreover, of a truth that has been verified by several studies: Rarely does an institution survive the death of its founder. If it does survive, either its animating spirit fades or it develops along new lines, inspired by the new leader. The best that rules can accomplish is preserve an organization in a state of suspended animation. "An institution," Emerson said, "is the lengthened shadow of one man."

An excellent example of rules written to preserve an institution's spirit may be seen in the traditional Christian monasteries. The monks and nuns who after centuries are still inspired in their way of life are those who have read, studied, and absorbed the spirit of their founders. Though bonded by the rules of their order, their real inspiration comes even today from the example of saints such as Francis and Clare of Assisi, and Teresa of

Avila. Without those wise and compassionate souls, the monasteries would long ago have become—as indeed many have become—spiritual mausoleums.

Saint Francis of Assisi is an interesting example. He recognized the stultifying effect of too many rules. Certain high dignitaries of the church in Rome, and a few monks in his own order, considering themselves more knowledgeable in practical matters than he, urged him, over his resistance, to write a rule; they insisted one was needed. Francis, anxious that rules not jeopardize the spirit of the order, agreed reluctantly, then wrote a document that was more poetic than legalistic. It was not found satisfactory. Francis tried again; indeed, he made several attempts. Nothing he wrote met with official approval. At last, all his versions were conveniently lost. Another document was substituted that contained all the careful provisos they'd wanted. It was, they felt, what the dignity of their great order demanded.

I do not say that systems are unnecessary. Common sense tells us they are essential. Yet it is interesting to note that, while the great teachers of mankind gave precepts and admonitions, they created no actual regulations. Jesus Christ told his disciple Peter, "Feed my sheep." He didn't say, "Organize them." It was his followers and others after them who created the church, and in so doing showed more interest in establishing control over the "sheep" than in feeding them.

Buddha is remembered for his teachings, not for an institution. The same is true for Lao-tse. There have been exceptions, but no teacher of that high caliber went so far as to say, "My Rule will suffice." Saint Benedict wrote a rule for monasteries as a reaction to years of monastic lack of discipline, and to the chaos that ravaged the world of his day. Organizers like him, however, hadn't the wisdom to see that form cannot ensure the spirit, or even nourish it. All it can do is facilitate the *expression* of spirit.

In the history of nations we see that, as the wave of civilization has passed from country to country, it has never been limited to specific forms. Nor has form ever taken the place of a culture's spirit. Rome's power declined over time despite the precision of its organization. *Pax Romana* endured only as long as Rome's spirit retained freshness and vitality. And then—the barbarians.

Where, now, the wonders of ancient Greece? Where, the mighty kingdom of the pharaohs? The hills of Greece may still be seen; so also the sands of Egypt. In both places, there are also a few impressive monuments. But the spirit? The poet Shelley memorialized the broken statue of Rameses II, at Luxor, in his famous poem, "Ozymandias." Civilization, despite the elaborate systems by which men have sought to preserve it, has passed on from land to land. Where it has endured the longest, it has not been structured by rigid rules, but animated by a vital and resilient outlook on life.

Every tradition loses vitality, eventually. Legends keep the flame alive for a time, but even those fade eventually to dying embers, and then ashes. A friend of mine who had been in the Marine Corps during the Korean War told me about a group of Texan recruits. "They loudly boasted," he said, "that they, Texan cowboys all—at least in their own minds—would beat everyone else when it came to rifle practice. The joke of it," he concluded with a laugh, "was that, of the various states represented, the Texans came out the worst!"

Legend is a sustaining power in the monastic life also. Twenty years ago I visited the island of Patmos. Two Greek Orthodox monasteries are situated there, one for men and the other for women. As I stood in line waiting for a ship to carry me and others back to the mainland, I chatted with a French couple standing in front of me. The lady exclaimed, "I conversed with some of the nuns. Their life is so simple, but, ah, what peace they emanate!"

"Really?" I answered, mildly surprised. "I spoke with some of the monks, but I must say I didn't feel any special peace in their presence."

The lady paused a moment, then to my amusement replied, "Come to think of it, I didn't really feel much peace from the nuns, either. It's just that I thought peace was what I ought to be feeling!"

The United States Constitution is surely one of

the great documents in history. England's Prime Minister Gladstone wrote in reference to it, "It is the most wonderful work ever struck off at a given time by the brain and purpose of man." The United States Supreme Court, however, working as conscientiously "by the book" as it can, has made rulings that would, one suspects, have caused the Founding Fathers to shudder, sensing betrayal.

Leonardo da Vinci had students help him with some of the detail work in his paintings. Presumably he taught them everything he could of his art. But there is no record that he communicated greatness to any of them.

Thousands of students, again, attend art school every year, and music school, and schools of architecture, and other schools where various sorts of skills are taught. No school has ever imparted genius. Very few graduates have become even passably good artists, or composers, or whatever else they've studied to be. On the other hand, not a few outstanding figures in those fields have become great without the benefit of formal schooling. It isn't that their methods, as a consequence of this lack, were haphazard. Obviously, judging by what they produced, they worked hard at their métier— perhaps all the harder for having had to learn so much on their own. Their inspiration, however, came from insights that could never have been conveyed to them in the classroom. Mere mechanisms have no life of their own: they are only a semblance of life. Inspiration is living; it conveys an actual consciousness.

The West, especially, has sought perfection through formal systems. This has not been the case everywhere. In ancient China, it is said, the emperors when touring their provinces would make a point wherever they went of listening to the music. They didn't first investigate the honesty of the officials. In each province it was the music that gave them what they considered to be a true picture of how things were going. If the melodies and cadences were right, they were satisfied that the right spirit prevailed. But if the music was in some way wrong, they were certain that error had crept also into the system. In such cases, in addition to making necessary adjustments in the administration, the emperors worked to correct the music. When melody and cadence were right, they believed, everything else would flow rightly also.

What an intriguing concept! Naturally, one receives it with a certain reservation. (Consider only the bluster with which an emperor, heir to an ancient tradition, would have been likely to comport himself if he was tone deaf. There is fertile material, here, for a comic opera!) Still, even accepting that the facts have probably been idealized, there is truth in the story. Fiction, in its symbolism, is sometimes truer than prosaic fact.

China lost its ancient principles with the passing of time—inevitably so, for ascent and descent are equally part of the nature of things. No more can be done about it than about an ocean's tossing waves. To give priority to systems, however, rather than to their animating consciousness, deprives even the best system, in time, of life. Without a sustaining consciousness, the form may survive, but only in a petrified state.

In utopian books starting with Plato's *Republic* (which is the earliest one I know), systems are presented as the key to a community's success. Thus, invariably, whenever a new community is proposed, such questions are asked as: "How will it work? What rules will it follow? How will its government be set up? How will decisions be made? What mechanism will ensure that decisions are enforced? How can the members be persuaded to work together harmoniously? How will the leaders be induced to serve others, rather than act for their own advantage? How will slackers be made more productive, and discouraged from taking advantage of others' good will? What provisions will there be for members who want to leave? How will the old or ailing be taken care of?"

In the very effort to meet such contingencies, people lose themselves in a labyrinth of rules and provisos. While these are to some extent necessary, they are not in themselves the way to meet even perfectly reasonable concerns. The truest answer to each of the above questions lies in developing a charitable spirit, primarily through example. If any community decides rules are essential to its actual spirit, rather than a simple mechanism for the expression of that spirit, it might do well to reserve space in a cemetery—not yet existent, of course, though not such a bad idea—for communities!

Years ago, in my own activity with groups, I had to recognize at last that group dynamics depend above all on right attitude. This attitude depends on the leader, since it is he, or she, who must instill it in the group. Rules may facilitate the flow of energy, but if too many rules are imposed they obstruct that flow. With right attitude, everything else follows naturally: efficiency, ability, even "practical know-how."

A dancer, to know how to execute a difficult step, must have the right "feeling," inwardly. A skier knows what to do with hips, knees, and elbows when the movements proceed from a consciousness that is centered in the spine. Economic skills, business skills, real estate skills, managerial skills: All of these flow naturally, without much effort, once a group's spirit is what it should be.

People with already-developed skills may also be attracted to a community as members. Experts, however, are not always the good fortune people might suppose. For there isn't any "one right way" of doing anything. Traditionally accepted ways often manifest a no-longer-acceptable spirit. Once the flow of energy is right, which it can be only when the consciousness behind it is right, its way of self-manifestation will be naturally compatible with that flow. Despite the scoffing of people steeped in old ways, the new ways, in a new context, will often be more effective. Thus, even if no trained people are attracted—and the emphasis should in any case be on the right spirit; skills are secondary—the members themselves may actually be better off. They can develop abilities and invent new ways of doing things. Skill, moreover, must never be made the standard of success. Otherwise, what will emerge is a lifeless form.

Back to those questions about system and provisos: The true answer to all of them is as I said: right attitude; above all, charity. When a community's members are men and women of good will, they won't need rules to bind them to what ought, then, to be a smoothly working system anyway. Custom, without commandments, will suffice. On the other hand, when good will is absent, no mere rule will ever compensate for that lack. Right attitude cannot be learned from books. It can only be absorbed by a kind of osmosis, from living examples—or else, self-generated.

In the West especially—though the penchant is common everywhere—so much emphasis is placed on mechanisms that the role of consciousness is often overlooked. Pygmalion's statue of a beautiful woman would have remained merely a piece of carved stone had not the goddess Aphrodite infused life into it, producing Galatea. Everything one does acquires life only to the extent that we *infuse* life—that is to say, energy—into it, directed by our consciousness.

In this book we have studied several presentations from the standpoint of their focus on mechanisms. To Adam Smith, economics was a purely material consideration. The nature of wealth wasn't something he thought needed refining. To him, paraphrasing Hegel, "All that is real is tangible, and all that is tangible is real."

Charles Darwin explained evolution also from a purely mechanical point of view. This was his entire explanation for how life arrived at its present level of complexity. The mechanics of natural selection sufficed, in his mind, to explain everything.

As I wrote in Chapter Two on Copernicus— And yet . . . and yet . . . :

A few cracks have begun to appear in Darwin's carefully constructed mechanism. No one so far, for example, has actually proved that there ever was a "missing link" between the lower forms of life and *Homo sapiens.* In spite of universal confidence that the link would be found, and in spite of a world-wide search for more than 150 years, the investigation so far has drawn a blank. Eagerness for recognition has produced a few fakes, but nothing provably genuine. Is this fact not surprising, considering what great zeal has been shown for the search?

Take another example: For a long time, mutations were the proposed explanation for how life evolves to new forms. So far, however, proof is virtually non-existent. Mutations appear almost invariably to be degenerate forms of their species. No mutation has shown itself to be meaningful— that is to say, advantageous in the struggle for survival. A cow with five legs is in no way better equipped than her four-legged sisters; probably she is at a disadvantage.

However, since Darwin's doctrine would probably remain entrenched anyway, it seems pointless to track to its lair this interesting lacuna in evolutionary theory.

In my book *Out of the Labyrinth,* I devoted four chapters to Darwinian evolution. Many years of thought and research went into writing that book. In those four chapters I said (as I've done here) that what Darwin gave us was a mere mechanism. As to the *motivation* behind it, this he reduced as much as possible to a blind, instinctual urge. Thus, he removed almost entirely the element of intelligence, replacing it with something as nearly mechanical as was possible for him. Thus has every natural scientist since Galileo and Newton tried to promote his field of study to the dignity of the purely material sciences, like physics.

In *Out of the Labyrinth* I discussed also the role of intelligence in evolution. For example, I pointed out that a leopard born with spots to an unspotted breed in the desert would not necessarily be at a disadvantage. Darwinian theory says it would be, for a leopard that was more visible to its intended prey than its fellows would be less capable of surviving. The leopard, however, is an intelligent animal. Finding itself with spots in a sandy environment, it would simply seek a better location such as in a jungle. The mechanics of evolution tell us only that a spotted leopard would have a harder time hunting in the desert. The leopard, however—canny enough, as we all know, to approach its prey from downwind—would surely also be intelligent enough to move away from disadvantageous surroundings. Its subsequent successful survival in the jungle will have been caused not only by the mutation that gave it birth. Rather, the leopard's intelligence, in moving to the jungle, will have directed the evolution of its species.

There is another anomaly in Darwin's theory. Human beings—if we accept the struggle for survival as the entire explanation—would not require a brain so much larger than that of any other animal. If survival were everything, people would need only sufficient cunning to outwit creatures less intelligent than themselves. Therefore, man's brain wouldn't have needed to evolve to its present size.

The very recognition, moreover, that intelligence is what has enabled man to survive in the "evolutionary sweepstakes" is proof sufficient that evolution is guided by motivation. The struggle is not blindly instinctive. Evolution, therefore, is not a mere mechanism. It is conscious and self-determined. The very wish to survive is an expression of consciousness.

Some may say that the explanation for the size of man's brain is that he has developed it in competition with his fellow human beings. Even in this case, the facts, which by no means indicate a mere mechanism, don't suggest a history of competition. Competition has always been there, of course, but the brain size of people all over the world is more or less the same. If competition were the explanation for its present size, we should see people with various sizes of brain in different parts of the world, especially in isolated areas.

Scientists tell us, moreover, that human beings rarely use more than a fraction of their potential brain power. Actual intelligence doesn't seem to vary even with people's skull capacity. Rather, it is evident that it depends on the *use* they make of their intelligence.

A book I touched on in Chapter Two, *The Hidden History of the Human Race* by Michael A.

Cremo and Richard L. Thompson,* gives abundant evidence that *Homo sapiens* has been around much longer than the accepted figure in orthodox anthropology. Could this much greater antiquity, if accepted, become another crack in the mechanism of Darwinian evolution?

Intelligence is, certainly, an important factor in evolution. I don't suppose Darwin himself would have denied it. He devoted so much space, however, to presenting evidence for his mechanical structure that by the time conscious intelligence intruded on the scene it no doubt seemed to him an anomaly not requiring mention. Obviously, species that can outwit their natural enemies are more fit to survive than those which cannot. Darwin, however, wasn't concentrating on the part played by intelligence in directing evolution. Perhaps it struck him as a mere bagatelle, by the time he'd overwhelmed his readers with that wealth of research.

In light of our present argument, however, intelligence deserves to be given primary importance. As George Gaylord Simpson, the renowned biologist, declared, there is "good concrete evidence for the

---

*Govardhan Hill Publishing, Badger, CA (1994). Everyone has a bias of some kind, though a fair-minded writer tries not to be affected by his own. Cremo and Thompson have an unorthodox religious commitment, one with which I must confess I am not wholly in tune, but their assessments seem to me objective. The facts they present have impressed numerous professionals, among them archaeologists, biologists, and other reputable scientists. On this basis alone, I think their book deserves an honest hearing. Personally, I found it fascinating.

impression that some animals have evolved much faster than others. There is less complete but still sufficient evidence for the further generalization that the vertebrates [animals with greater intelligence] have tended to evolve (structurally) faster than the invertebrates."*

A final question follows close upon those conclusions: If intelligence affects the evolutionary process, why hasn't the human race, of all species the most intelligent, continued to evolve at a faster rate—physically, but even more particularly in intelligence? Physically, there have been only very minor changes in the human body, and virtually no change in the size of man's brain. Intelligence among human beings, it's true, has little to do with brain size. (The brain capacity of Cro-Magnon man is said to have been larger than modern man's, but no evidence has been found that his intelligence was superior to our own.) However, there isn't any other evidence, either, of overall increase in individuals' intelligence. If, indeed, humankind is continuing to evolve, in what does that evolution consist, and what is its cause? Traditional accounts in terms of "survival of the fittest" don't appear to offer any explanation.

Darwin, even more than Machiavelli and Adam Smith, shocked people into accepting that life must be defined in terms of fierce competition. People

---

The Meaning of Evolution (Yale University Press, New Haven, Conn., 1949).

had already been conditioned to view it as a struggle for power, based on self-interest. Since Darwin, life has come to seem like a struggle for more than power: for sheer survival, a dog-eat-dog existence in which only the fittest live, and any threat to one's own power must be destroyed, the "unfit" eliminated in order that the strong may stand proudly at the top of the dung heap. The victors in this war are the predators. "Lambs" serve only to provide food. The more ruthless, self-centered, and callous a person is, the greater his chances of survival. Nothing matters, but survival.

What an appalling picture! The result has been delusions like the Nazi "master race," with what was their version of a "manifest destiny" of world dominion. It has been Marxist communism with its supposed class struggle, leading to the butchery of millions in the name of "survival of the fittest." Darwin attributed no more meaning to life than material science has to the universe. But what people took from his theory was a new conception of life's meaning: the ruthless struggle to survive at all costs.

Most of the theories considered in this book are not issues of fact, but only of interpretation. The facts Darwin presented are not challenged here. His *interpretation,* however, was suggested to him not by the facts, but by the way he'd been conditioned to think. In a more benign intellectual climate, he'd have seen things very differently. He might, for instance, have seen evolution as a constant search for *opportunities* for the "life urge" to express itself more fully.

If, however, intelligence and motivation are admitted to be factors in evolution (as we've argued they should be), then fitness for survival is less of an issue particularly where human beings are concerned. Nor is it even a major focus of people's attention and energy. A person's self-evaluation, and the contribution he makes to society, depend not nearly so much on survival as they do on countless other, and far more immediate, issues. Indeed, concern for physical survival as opposed to, say, the survival of a work of genius, could have made a fitting parody for the comic dramatist Molière, or for a Gilbert and Sullivan operetta. I can imagine a Darwinist looking at a painting titled "The Triumph of Light over Darkness" and snorting, "Bah! What's that got to do with surviving?"

Even intelligence falls short of being the whole story. What we see in evolution, rather, is the unfolding of *consciousness.* People themselves are not nearly so much concerned with surviving as they are with consciously living and enjoying their lives. Of course, if a person finds his life threatened, his instinct for self-preservation will cry for attention and will perhaps overwhelm all other considerations. That instinct won't necessarily win out, however. For in the very face of death one may consciously override it. Socrates demonstrated this kind of transcendence when he was condemned to death by the rulers of Athens. He could have escaped; his friends urged him to do so. Yet, true to what he felt was his higher duty, he voluntarily swallowed the poisonous hemlock.

Many other people, similarly, have transcended the instinct for survival by remaining true to what they felt to be a higher duty. Consider the Christian martyrs, willingly accepting death. The choice to die is sometimes exhibited even by lower animals.

When I was a child, a friend of my family's was leaving her house accompanied by her German shepherd. Just at that moment, a mad dog entered the garden gate. Her pet knew it would have no chance of surviving the intruder's bite. It also knew that it might escape and leave its owner to her fate. Instead, and fully aware that it was helpless to defend itself, it stood calmly in front of the woman, blocking the mad dog's approach. The rabid creature bit it, then ran off barking crazily. I would like to be able to report that this act of heroism had a happy ending thanks to the wonders of modern medicine. Unfortunately, the German shepherd died, as evidently it had known it would. May we not say, however, that although it was a "mere" animal, it displayed a noble nature?

It isn't often, of course, that a person actually finds his life threatened. We *assume* life's continuance as normal to our existence; few of us even think about death. We don't anticipate that a venomous snake may strike at us out of the bushes we pass. We don't fear being run over by every passing car. Of course we take normal precautions against danger, if we recognize it as real, but to do so isn't an obsession with most of us. As long as we are alive, we are more interested in enjoying life than we are in preserving it.

Economists and social reformers describe existence among the poor as a sort of grey inferno. They overlook the amazing adaptability of human nature. I'm not insensitive to human suffering. In fact, I do what I can to alleviate it, when I find it. But I cannot be persuaded that survival alone is anybody's major concern, unless indeed he finds himself at death's door. I have seen beggar children whine with practiced pathos as they lamented not having eaten for three days, then run off gaily to play with their friends, a new quantity of coins clutched in their hands. I have seen sufferers dying in hospitals who felt deep pity for the sufferings of others, and who expressed gratitude for the lessons they had learned from their own trials. Darwin's mechanisms of evolution completely by-pass these very human realities. To the scientist, they lack biological significance. They do not, however, lack *human* significance.

Darwin was so wholly focused on struggle as the explanation for evolution that he gave no thought to what it is that survives the struggle. If his own survival had been at stake, however, I'm sure he'd have resolutely finished his magnum opus even against his doctor's strictest orders. We, as human beings, are more concerned with our own state of awareness—our joy, or our pain—than we are with evolutionary mechanisms. For us, our bodies are, above all, instruments through which we express our thoughts, feelings, and awareness. Were we to lose a limb, we'd manage somehow to adjust, and probably even happily, after a period of mental adjustment. When we speak with a crippled person, it is his *consciousness* we address, not his mutilated body. He remains for us a living human being, not a damaged machine.

It is this aspect of Darwinism that leaves a sour taste in the mouth. Biologists are, of course, interested in how it all came about mechanically, and one assumes Darwin's explanation for that "how" is acceptably accurate. He doesn't explain consciousness, however, which is far more interesting to us as human beings. Biologists, attempting to remain sternly "objective," sneer at the very question of consciousness. To them it demonstrates an unscientific bias.

"Has man changed more," asked James F. Crow in *Scientific American* (in its September, 1959, issue) "in developing his brain than the elephant has by growing a trunk?" Crow was convinced it shows prejudice to consider "mere consciousness" as important. We survive, he insisted, if we can; nothing else matters. The question, however, cannot but arise in the mind: What do we survive *for?*

For the past several centuries, mechanisms have been raised virtually to the level of a creed. Had Adolf Hitler won World War II he would have hailed that victory as proof that the "pure" Germanic stock was the fittest to survive. Muscled arrogance in that case would have been touted as the peak of human achievement. In such "perfection," however, gorillas could easily have outshone human beings.

Mechanisms were Adam Smith's premise in *The Wealth of Nations.* They were Plato's in *The Republic* with his so-called "perfect" society. They were the point of More's *Utopia,* of Francis Bacon's *New Atlantis,* of Machiavelli's *The Prince.* They were the whole point of William Harvey's treatise on blood circulation. (Medical science today, it is interesting to note, has discovered that the heart actually possesses intelligence; it is by no means merely a blood-pumping organ.*) The discoveries of Copernicus, of Tycho Brahe, Kepler, Galileo, and Newton only probed into the mechanics of the universe; they didn't ponder the purpose behind it. It wasn't that they denied the existence of such a purpose. In fact, most of them, perhaps all, believed there is one. They initiated a direction of thinking, however, that led others to the conclusion that purpose is nonexistent.

*See, for example, Doc Childre and Howard Martin, The Heart-Math Solution (HarperCollins Publishers Inc., New York City, 1999).

Marx and Engels based their whole philosophy on the premise of social evolution as a mechanism. Thomas Malthus, in his *Essay on the Principle of Population,* showed the mechanical limitations of population growth.

Malthus, incidentally—I made this point earlier, but it bears repetition here—predicted disaster for humanity. Population growth, he said, will inexorably exceed the earth's capacity to feed everyone. As he pointed out, it is human nature to breed. Population will always, according to him, increase by geometric progression, whereas the food available can increase only arithmetically, and must eventually fail to keep pace with population increase. His prediction of mass starvation seems reasonable even today, though scientific achievements continue to defer the day of reckoning. That doom cannot, however, according to his argument, be averted forever. Would scientific technology be able to feed, let us say, 100 billion people, rather than the present six billion? Quite possibly not.

Earlier, however, we considered another factor: Economically progressive nations no longer match the Malthusian curve of continued population growth. In fact, most of them have already reached a plateau, producing fewer children than the poor nations. It frequently happens, in fact, that the well-to-do classes in every nation produce fewer children, generally speaking, than the poor ones. In wealthier countries the population, at present, is either stable or is actually declining. Apart from the explanations usually given for this disparity—the lack, for example, of proper education among the poor in methods of birth control—one cannot help suspecting a further reason: Life affords fewer opportunities to the poor for enjoyment, other than sexual indulgence. Surely, a simple solution to the problem of over-population would be to raise the level of prosperity everywhere. This possibility, rather than scientific technology applied directly to the problem, is—given present-day progress in so many fields—at least imaginable.

A further solution may be considered also. Small, intentional communities are less likely to produce large numbers of children than the population elsewhere, most of which define life by their material desires and pleasures. People who live by high ideals concentrate on ends that are not merely commercial. The effect on them will be similar to that of prosperity in nations: Their energy will be directed more toward those ideals, and less toward producing progeny. Though such communities will likely be small, their general influence, because concentrated, will be out of all proportion to their size.

To what extent is Darwin's theory of evolution relevant to daily life as we live it? Of particular interest is the question: Is evolution an upward thrust from below, in reaction to the challenge to survival? Or can it be explained even more satisfactorily as a pull from above? People think of God, if

He exists, as somewhere "up there," perhaps in outer space. But what about the conscious will to perfection, which is a factor in every human life? Isn't that, for human needs, a sufficient definition of divinity—not something outside oneself, but a higher, though dimly intuited, potential? Is there, in other words, an aspect of consciousness itself that seeks fulfillment in a greater, more expanded awareness?

If one were to judge a building before its walls had been raised, wouldn't he be considered a trifle hasty? "Wait a bit!" the builder would remonstrate, quite understandably. "I haven't finished my job!" Evolution, too, may be simply a work in progress— its advancement determined not by some all-powerful deity, but by an innate impulse at the heart of every living creature. Biologists tell us that evolution is simply a process without meaning, lacking in any purpose or direction. Naturally, if mechanism is the only issue, one shouldn't even concern himself with asking, "Why?" The mechanic asks simply, "How?"

"Why," however, is a question that arises naturally in the mind.

In *Out of the Labyrinth,* I described several twentieth-century experiments for which there are only two possible alternatives, mutually exclusive. Convincing evidence has been found to suggest that no dividing line exists between animate and inanimate matter. Metals, for instance, have been shown repeatedly to respond to stimuli in the same way that living tissues respond. Scientists, accepting this data (it is convincing), conclude that this means everything is without either life (as we think of it) or consciousness. Consciousness, they assert, is only a materially produced phenomenon: an outcome of the movement of electrons in the brain. Life, they say, is only a movement of energy in coherent organisms.

The blurred distinctions, however, between the living and the non-living suggest ineluctably another alternative: namely, that *everything* is conscious, however dimly so. Could it be that some sort of inchoate awareness exists even in the rocks and minerals?

In an age when consciousness itself is assumed to be only a product of brain activity, the suggestion that awareness, even latent, may exist in everything seems bizarre. On the other hand, to conclude that nothing is conscious is to ignore the obvious fact that it takes *consciousness* to reach such a conclusion!

When ether was first proposed over two centuries ago, as the medium through which light travels in space, it seemed to everyone a satisfactory explanation. New discoveries, however, kept forcing more and more re-evaluations. At last, the whole structure of theory had to be abandoned: It was simply too cumbersome to be of any use.

Science, similarly, has plodded along without

giving much thought to such subtleties as consciousness. Its focus has been on what it could observe, physically. It is consciousness, however, that does the observing. René Descartes, in addressing the question of existence, felt it necessary to identify consciousness with thinking. "I think," he said, "therefore I am (*Cogito, ergo sum*)." He was mistaken, however. Thinking is not necessary to consciousness. He didn't take consciousness into account for the reason that consciousness, unlike thought, was not something he could observe with scientific objectivity.

A joke has it that Descartes entered a bar, and the bartender asked him if he'd like a beer. "I think not," replied Descartes—and disappeared!

On a more serious note, we've all had moments, surely, when we weren't thinking, but were intensely aware. The enjoyment of music, or absorption in the sight of a beautiful sunset: these experiences may have kept us without a thought for moments together. Our awareness, moreover, was probably more intense when our thoughts were at rest. Descartes was mistaken. It must be added, however, that he was not alone in his error. It was natural to anyone trained, as he had been, in scientific methodology. Science teaches that if a thing can't be observed, it isn't a fit subject for investigation, and may not even exist.

Whether or not everything is conscious, it is certainly true that the development of consciousness is an aspect of the evolutionary process. Intelligence is demonstrably so. A monkey that discards a banana to pick up and chew on a nut isn't thinking about survival: It is simply expressing curiosity. It is also doing so intelligently, with a desire for conscious enjoyment.

Consider a certain type of mollusc, which rubs itself repeatedly back and forth against a rock until, after fifteen years, it creates a niche deep enough to settle into. This movement may rank so low on the scale of awareness as not even to be considered intelligent. Who can deny, however, that there is consciousness in the movement? Nothing external acts upon the mollusc to produce that simple motion. Tides, waves, wind, alterations of temperature: none of these. Its action is generated entirely from within. We would gain nothing by testing the mollusc's intelligence. Without testing it, we may assume fairly safely that probably it would flunk any such test. Yet the mollusc is aware, obviously, not insensate; active, not inert.

Mankind, too, in reaching out toward ideals that inspire it, is not expressing a merely mechanistic urge. It is man's consciousness that reaches out. Although we haven't evolved much, physically, since our first entrance on the stage of life, we have changed mentally, morally, and spiritually— upwards, downwards, or sideways depending on each person's attitudes toward life.

To return to our theme: Small, intentional communities, where people live and work closely together, represent a conscious resolution on their part to reach out toward some new and better way of living, some more vital way of interacting with others and of fulfilling their aspirations. Intentional communities are not an accident of social evolution, nor are they a product of Marxian brooding: They are an evolutionary expression of individual aspiration.

It would be a mistake to press upon the reader any particular community system. Numerous possibilities exist for expressing the same basic principles. I have not even pressed upon readers the fact that I myself have actually founded several successful communities. They are still thriving, after more than thirty years, and, taken all together, contain nearly a thousand members. The issue, however, is not what, specifically, has been done, or what might be done. Rather, it is the exhilarating realization that in this concept near-virgin territory awaits exploration. The possibilities are vast, like those of a new continent. I invite you to explore this concept for yourself. All you need is the willingness to begin, and the awareness that success depends on resolute vision and willingness. Everything else will follow, from that initial determination.

CHAPTER NINE

❋

Human Evolution

We have seen that mankind hasn't evolved much, physically speaking, since the first human beings appeared on this planet. On every other level, however—in mental, cultural, and spiritual outlook, for example—man's development in all directions, as single individuals and as societies, has been astonishing. Darwin didn't describe evolution as necessarily upward, and I am not referring to human evolution as progressive, either. Changes, however, of outlook, tastes, and interests have included as much variety as man's imagination can conceive.

The lower animals haven't shown anything like such flexibility. The legend, still visible on the gate of a home in ancient Pompeii, reads, "*Cave canem* (beware of the dog)." The same warning may be seen on homes today throughout the world. I suspect also that the canine penchant for running after moving vehicles has not changed in thousands of years. Cats may disdain those functions (though history actually does provide a few bizarre instances of "guard cats," perhaps made so by trainers' ingenuity), but as far as I know cats have always been comfortable with their role as mousers.

Human beings are unpredictable. In this sense they are like the hedgehogs in Alice in Wonderland, which, though supposed to act as balls in a croquet game, kept uncurling themselves and wandering off in different directions. Each human being is, simply, himself. He can rise or fall; grow more intelligent or less so (or even stupid); he can develop tastes he never had before, or lose those he once thought defined him; become kindly, or aggressive; calm, or nervous. It is true that there is an essential "I" in everyone that never changes. This fact can be seen in the eyes of a child in a photograph, for example, compared to those of the old man he is now, sixty years later. In their behavior, however, people can develop tendencies far removed from any they displayed as children.

Modern psychology has tried to arrest this colorful process by confining human nature in a little cage of definitions. Carl Jung divided people into introverts and extroverts. Alfred Adler explained the need to excel as a compensation for what he called the "inferiority complex." Sigmund Freud, the father of modern psychology, claimed that the libido, or sex drive, is man's fundamental reality. All three men, indeed, were only following a trail that science had blazed already, with its insistence on defining everything possible—as though to freeze the fluctuations of reality in still poses in order to understand and work with them better. Human beings can't be pinned to a board, however, like butterflies. To confine them in fixed roles is to prevent the further development of their own nature. Even butterflies are pinned only after they are dead. In a living butterfly, who at any moment can predict the direction in which it will fly next?

One theme runs like a thread through all the writings we've been considering: *competition.* Machiavelli pitted rulers against their subjects. Adam Smith claimed that the highway to national wealth is free competition in the marketplace. Competition was what Thomas Malthus discerned between population growth and the earth's ability to feed its inhabitants. Hegel defined progress as a dialectic—a competition, in other words, between opposite concepts, and a resulting synthesis. Darwin's concept of natural selection, from which followed the Darwinist concept of a struggle for survival—a competition between species—was the basis for his theory of evolution. From there it was a short step to Karl Marx and Friedrich Engels with their theory of class struggle which, again, included competition. And, finally, it was natural that this line of development should lead to Sigmund Freud, explorer of the one remaining field in this long progression: the human mind.

Freud discerned *within* human beings the competition others had observed outwardly. He defined the nature and origins of man's inner conflicts, or "complexes," and then set out to show people how they might resolve them. It may be added that there is in his writings a hint of almost Wagnerian hyperbole.

Biological evolution, as Darwin explained it, lacks any discernible purpose. All it demonstrates is the endlessly prolific exuberance of Nature. Freud saw psychological evolution, similarly, as having no meaning. He invented psychoanalysis to help people develop a normal life. This normality, however, was as far as he went toward suggesting there was any meaning in life. Like the other authors before him, he was interested in the way things worked, not in why they worked that way. That is to say, he didn't think in terms of people's own aspirations, or of how he might help them to achieve those goals in their lives. What, then, constituted for him a normal life? He didn't say. It doesn't seem even to have occurred to him to say. His reasoning was simply that if people can be released from their repressions, they will be better able to cope rationally with their existence.

The technique Freud created for gaining release from repression is known as "free association." The patient reclines on a couch in a dimly lighted room, and gives random utterance to a so-called "stream of consciousness." Months of such outpouring produce data through which the psychoanalyst culls for meaningful insight.

Freud also analyzed dreams, which he claimed

reveal a person's repressions and unfulfilled desires. Needless to say, truly to comprehend this kind of data requires great sensitivity. Intellectual analysis is not enough. The psychoanalyst must be sympathetic also—even intuitive, if possible. Unfortunately, the word *analysis* suggests a purely intellectual activity. Given the direction modern thought has taken, any other kind of diagnosis would appear unscientific. New words were indicated, and a host of ponderous definitions—the more abstract, the better!

Deep feelings, however, cannot be understood by the intellect alone, any more than a song can be understood by analyzing the singer's facial expressions. True insight demands sensitive feeling in the heart. Calm feeling, indeed, is far more important than aloof analysis for understanding people. Many, no doubt, enter the psychiatric profession from a desire to help others. Nevertheless, the training they receive conditions the development of an intellectual outlook, and a lessening of empathy, for the sake of maintaining scientific objectivity.

I had an amusing dream recently. It was just before waking in the morning. I was supposed to play a trombone solo with Glenn Miller's band. I've never played the trombone, and in my dream had never done so, either. I blew a few tentative notes, first, and was mildly surprised when they came out passably well. The band members smiled in appreciation for my effort; one of them called out, "All right!" They were friendly and supportive, though certainly not overly impressed by my ability. Before I could blow another note, it turned out I was to sing a well-known Glenn Miller number, "Chattanooga Choo-Choo," with Glenn Miller himself singing the introduction. We were in a studio, not on stage before an audience. Song sheets were spread out before us on a piano top, and the pianist was about to begin playing when I woke up.

Now then, what can this dream mean? Glenn Miller's was perhaps the best-known band in the early 1940s. He played the trombone superbly. A tie-in comes to mind: Two days earlier, I had noticed the name "At Last" on a brochure for a new medical device. "At Last" was also the name of a song Glenn Miller recorded many years ago for a movie. A fairly tenuous link, but there you have it.

Looking at my dream from a Freudian perspective, I can imagine a psychoanalyst saying that it portrayed wish fulfillment, or, otherwise, a fear of appearing foolish in public. Would either analysis be correct? There was no audience in the dream; therefore that particular fear was not likely. In fact, I wasn't fearful. The band members were all friendly toward me, and in no way opposed to making it happen. Was I emotionally engaged in any way: nervous? apprehensive? competitive? overconfident? eager to show off? happy to be in the company of a famous person with such a prominent band? worried about how the public might receive me? pleased with the music? displeased with anything? concerned about my ability to perform well? No, none of the above. I was simply interested, not emotionally involved. As far as I can tell, the whole thing had no meaning at all. When I awoke, there remained only amusement at this quite trivial episode.

A psychoanalyst, however, might see promising possibilities in my dream. I've said it contained no hint of wish fulfillment: But (the psychoanalyst might ask skeptically), am I being really honest with myself? I've said I felt no apprehension: But (he might wonder), am I perhaps fooling myself? I've said I had no dread of the public's reaction: But (the psychoanalyst might well remind me), fear of appearing in public, especially as a speaker or a performer, is said to be one of humanity's three greatest phobias. So then—who knows?

I imagine one could ferret out any number of "revelations" in that dream, were one so inclined. Yet when I awoke, I was only amused. I would have dismissed it from my mind had it not occurred to me that the dream might make an interesting addition to this chapter. A psychoanalyst, relying on intellect alone, might have much to say on the subject, but if he considered my own feelings in the matter—and after all it *was* my dream!—I think he'd close his notebook and seek elsewhere for clues as to the *real* Don Walters.

As I contemplate dreams I've found meaningful

in my life—this wasn't one of them!—it seems to me that their message often was not so much in their literal content as in the feeling that lingered with me afterward. Sometimes this feeling conveyed a clear message. Not infrequently, the feeling had little bearing on the actual dream events. What mattered was that I awoke with some fresh insight, some new resolution. Feelings like these are subjective and personal; I wouldn't want people picking them apart. What those dreams accomplished for me was significant for their results, not for my analysis of their contents.

A problem with free association was pointed out in 1942 by Ludwig Wittgenstein, the prominent Austrian-British philosopher, whose word for it was, *"queer."* "Freud," he said, "never shows . . . where to stop." Wittgenstein noted, in addition, that Freud never told his patients, "This is the right solution."

Psychoanalysis gives us no goal. Nor does it hold out a hope of what everyone desires most deeply: happiness. People are left more or less where Darwin dumped them: stuck in the mire of their animal origins with nowhere to go and nothing to hope for. If our ancestors were monkeys or lemurs or any other sort of lower species, and if we evolved to our present level only by accident, then to be human is not essentially different from being any other animal. It is in any case the same old struggle for survival. Our animal self is all that we really are, dressed up pretentiously in clothes. Indeed, to pursue recognition of that reality to the last degree of self-honesty, we should trace our fundamental reality back farther still: to the worms, the molluscs, the amebas.

What does it accomplish to tell ourselves that we are "only" animals? Darwinian thinking, by posing survival as the sole criterion of achievement, demands this admission. If the past is the only present reality, then aspiration of any kind is a delusion, for it bears no relation to that basic, unvarying question: survival.

Freud makes much of people's "animal" libido. Interestingly, many lower forms of life are asexual. In the higher animals, moreover, sexual expression is usually seasonal, not obsessive, as it can become in human beings. The conclusion is inescapable: Addiction to sex, for those who have it, comes not from their animal but from their human nature. With man's developed intelligence, his imagination can grow insatiable. Rarely do fetishes of this sort appear in lower animals.

Freud described the human psyche as existing on three levels: the Id, the Ego, and the Superego. The first of them, the id, he said reaches far back into our animal past. It is "the dark, inaccessible part of our personality," animal in nature, sexual, and unconscious. The id "contains everything that is inherited, that is present at birth, that is fixed in the constitution." It is blind and ruthless. (How many animals might be so described? Beetles, maybe! Certainly mammals demonstrate kindness also, and a sense of caring and consideration for one another. Any attempt to attribute mere "mechanism" to such behavior must be labeled pure, but not very reasonable, projection.) The sole impulse of the id, Freud said, is to gratify desires, careless of the consequences. The id has no values, and no moral sense.

Freud's next step up is the ego, which develops out of our awareness of the world around us, and in recognition of the need to curb the "blind and ruthless" tendencies of the id so as not to be in conflict with society's expectations of us.

The final level is the superego, which Freud said is our conscience. Conscience by his definition develops in response to the prohibitions and rules of conduct that are imposed upon us by society—by parents, teachers, and other authority figures in our lives.

Both the id and the superego, according to Freud, are unconscious. This is an infelicitous designation, for nothing connected with the mental processes can literally be unconscious. "*Sub*conscious" would be a better word, since these parts of the psyche are lower, not higher, than conscious awareness. The word, *subconscious,* has been available since Baron Leibniz in the seventeenth century and Kant in the eighteenth. Leibniz and Kant, however, associated the subconscious with mere peripheral awareness. Freud's "unconscious" descends to levels never even considered before, which fact, probably, explains why he felt a need to give them new names. In his designations, however, he opened the door to quasi-mystical, or at any rate unprovable, "intuitions"—the Wagnerian touch. Regardless how deep the id goes, it cannot be unconscious. Were it so, it simply wouldn't exist.

Freud is deservedly famous for having made people aware of the extent to which many of their mental processes lie out of sight of the wakeful state. To scorn his contribution would be like criticizing Christopher Columbus for not describing California. Nevertheless, it would be well also to realize that Freud was speaking less with the authority of long tradition and experience than as a pioneer. One ought not to expect him to be infallible.

The title of Chapter Four was, "Ask First: Does It Work?" That is what we must do with Freud's theories: ask first, Do they work?

Freud dealt largely with mental abnormalities. The important thing, to him, was to return his patients to an ability to function normally. What he offered them, however, was a boat without a rudder, which took them anywhere or nowhere as wind and ocean currents carried it. Since the only direction he proposed was the shore left behind, and no clear destination, people could only brood endlessly on their vague origins, and hack away at the rope which tied them to the shore. That shore, and the rope, were the only reality he suggested to them. Psychoanalysis, the method he invented, was supposed to help them sever that rope. After that, however, they were left adrift in a derelict vessel.

"The theory of repression," Freud wrote, "is the cornerstone on which the whole structure of psychoanalysis rests." One must seriously question whether release is really achieved by this negative approach. How could his patients be expected to leave something tangible (the life they knew) for something intangible and unknown (the unconscious Id)? Far more effective would be something more positive. For this approach, two alternatives suggest themselves: affirmation, and visualization.

Affirmation, to be effective, must be wholly positive. For example, never tell yourself, "I *will not* fail!" Say, rather, "I *will* succeed!" Again, self-correction shouldn't emphasize the difficulties. Don't tell yourself, "I have all this stuff inside me to process." Say, rather, "I will do everything I can to build a new life!"

Visualization should be practiced with the idea of reinforcing your ability to overcome. Imagine yourself, for example, standing on a lake shore. Mentally cast your inner obstacles, like salt crystals, into the clear water; watch them dissolve and disappear. Or visualize a bonfire and throw those obstacles, like ragged chips of wood, into the fire.

Watch them be consumed by flames of joy. Or, again, mentally touch those obstacles with a sparkler of joyful laughter.

Mental "tricks" like these will not be helpful to everyone, but the point in any case is to direct energy *away from* the obstacles and *toward* solution-consciousness. To concentrate on solutions is far more useful than letting oneself be sucked down in a whirlpool of problem-consciousness.

Clarity cannot be achieved so long as the emotions are disturbed. To calm them, don't try merely thinking your way out of them. Freud appealed to the intellect, but intellect alone is like a bark without a rudder. Today's reasoned "break-through" drifts two days later into a fog. One asks himself, "Now, what was that insight I had?" It was a gossamer! Thoughts fluctuate constantly. They need the guidance of strong feeling, otherwise they are evanescent. The feeling itself must be calm, moreover, otherwise it may easily be misleading. Calmness requires establishment at one's own center, and an end to jumping up and down at one's periphery.

These principles are important for intentional communities also. Their members may feel inclined to concentrate on their problems in the hope of finding solutions to them. The leaders may give priority also to helping the "problem" members, thinking to integrate them into the over-all better spirit. Progress in a community, however, comes by solution-consciousness, even as progressive self-understanding does in the individual. Goals can be achieved most easily by fully expecting them, and by working energetically, in a spirit of inner freedom, toward their achievement.

Nothing is served by devoting too much energy to members who are dissident or less supportive. There will always be a few, for those who begin with good intentions sometimes lose steam, once the novelty wears away. The best one may hope for from them is that whatever negative influence they have will be neutralized. Dissidents can't be expected to support something they themselves don't personally like. It is better to devote energy to members who support what is being done. Positive energy, like a magnet, attracts more positive energy. Negative energy, on the other hand, if addressed with excessive concern, can drain away positive energy.

In personal counseling, people should be advised not to concentrate too much on freeing themselves from inner conflicts. All they'll do in that process is nourish such conflicts by their fascination with them. Rather, suggest they set themselves some positive goal. This doesn't necessarily mean they should pretend that the conflicts don't exist. Indeed, awareness of a problem often awakens the energy needed to overcome it. But why go to all the trouble of ferreting them all out? The very attempt might take a lifetime. And the recognition would dawn at last that, in giving them so much attention, one hasn't energy left for positive accomplishment. Success comes almost always by maintaining solution-consciousness, and is actually *attracted* by positive expectations. But it is delayed indefinitely, if not actually repelled, by problem-consciousness.

An important question in this case, after asking, "Does it work?" is to ask, Has psychotherapy *ever* produced radiant, magnetic, outstandingly successful human beings? I am not aware that it has. The question, "Will it work?" should be applied not only to patients, but to psychoanalysts.

Freud wrote, "No psychoanalyst goes further than his own complexes and internal resistances permit." This statement begs for a look at the man himself, not only at his theories.

Sigmund Freud, according to his long-time friend and biographer Ernst Jones, had a good, if ironic, sense of humor. Despite the fact, moreover, that toward the end of his life he suffered greatly from jaw cancer, he was never heard to complain. These, certainly, are indications of a well-integrated personality.

On the other hand, Ernst Jones wrote also that Freud was obsessively concerned with death, especially with his own. Moreover, it distressed him deeply when a colleague contradicted his concepts, as happened in the falling out he had with Carl Jung and Alfred Adler. Freud's lack of objectivity in that disagreement—after all, he, too, was only a pioneer in that field—suggests an obsession with maintaining control. Obsessive behavior is suggested also by his preoccupation with death. Such an exaggerated fear must be considered neurotic. Freud himself, had he observed this fear in someone else, would surely have called it abnormal.

It may not be fair to read too much into photographs. Even so, the photos I've seen of Freud do not stir in me the thought, "I'd love to be like that man!" Rather, they show him dour, self preoccupied, and totally absorbed in his own theories. One derives no suggestion of that friendliness a person instinctively hopes to see in anyone from whom he'd like to receive guidance.

So then—no radiant patients; no radiant physician; no radiant results from the physician's methods. What is left? Psychoanalysis even today, of course, is still, relatively speaking, in its infancy. We should leniently judge those who work hard to develop this new field of knowledge, of all fields the most elusive. Psychiatry, moreover, has evolved greatly since its pioneering days. Though it still has a long way to go, one hopes that in time it will offer intuitive guidance to people seeking to achieve their own highest potential.

The greatest obstacle for psychiatrists has always been a temptation to arrogance. Wisdom is not so common anywhere as one would wish, being the fruit of maturity, not of a university education.

Wisdom depends above all on two things: humility, and sincere, deep feeling for others. It is important that psychoanalysis not become a new, surrogate religion. Were it so to become, the further evolution of understanding in that field would temporarily cease.

Years ago I had an instructive experience. I'd injured my vocal cords after leading a hundred people in singing while afflicted, myself, with a bad case of laryngitis. I'd protested I couldn't do it, but, faced with people's insistence, I'd relented. For months thereafter I'd had to rest my voice, during which time I visited several doctors. I was told that my vocal cords were ulcerated. Finally one doctor suggested I try speech therapy. I searched the yellow pages in the telephone directory, and found listed there a woman therapist whose office was near where I lived. It turned out she also practiced psychotherapy.

As I sat in her office, a man in the outer room waved to her on his way out, and called, "Goodbye." That was all. His tone of voice, however, his body language, his ingratiating smile: all these projected the message, "See, Mother, I'm much better now—aren't I?" He exuded immature dependence. I don't remember what she replied, but I do recall her manner at that moment. It was motherly and reassuring, as if to say, "You're doing just fine, dear." To my mind there was something vaguely distasteful in this episode. Here, I thought, was a grown man, not a child. To be "much better now" ought to have meant he was stronger in himself, not vaguely anxious for reassurance.

She closed the door, and asked me to lie down on a couch. Seated beside it, and leaning close, she asked me in a sugary tone, "What would you like me to call you?" I thought, Are you asking me to open my arms to you like a little child to its mommy? To be expected to trust someone so implicitly whom I'd never met before seemed to me wholly unreasonable. "You may call me Walters," I replied. "I never ask strangers to address me by my first name."* She backed off immediately. And so ended the only psychotherapy session I've ever had. Outside, afterward, a friend suggested I try chiropractic treatments. Two neck adjustments later, I was completely cured.

There seems to me something unwholesome about therapy that attempts to reduce the patient's confidence in himself and make him submissive and dependent on the therapist. It undermines his innate dignity. It isn't that I don't believe in humility. I believe in it very much. To accept a negative self-image, however, is not humility, for it leads to self-absorption, the very opposite of humility.

Humility means self-forgetfulness. It means to respect others, and out of that respect to refrain

---

*To clarify my statement, the reply I gave her was because she had asked that question. Otherwise, as far as I'm concerned people may call me what they like.

from intruding on them unless they extend an invitation. Even then, a certain distance, based on respect, smoothes communication even among friends, by keeping it non-invasive. Excessive familiarity is demeaning to true friendship.

My objection to psychoanalysis—as analysis only, not as wise inquiry—is that it encourages people to become self-centered. How can a person become inwardly free if his thoughts revolve incessantly around himself?

On a ship outside Norway once I had a conversation with a New York psychiatrist. He asked me, "How do you work with the people in your communities?"

"We encourage them," I replied, "to stand on their own two feet and not depend too much on others for help. We urge them not to focus on their shortcomings, or on how they've been treated by life or by others, but to work on developing their own clarity and strength."

To my astonishment, the man returned, "In other words, you're telling me you're the opposition!"

What a statement! And how demeaning, I thought, to his patients! Alas, psychiatry too often encourages victim-consciousness, as if trying to get patients to find freedom not even in self-confrontation, but in receiving kind treatment from others.

Not long ago I watched a video movie, *Pride and Prejudice,* based on the novel of that name by Jane

Austen. Featuring Greer Garson and Laurence Olivier in the leading roles, the movie contains a sequence that isn't in the novel, in which Mr. Darcy (Olivier) tries to teach Elizabeth Bennet (Garson) how to shoot a bow and arrow. Mr. Darcy doesn't realize it, but Elizabeth is much better at archery than he is. Her three shots all hit the bull's eye. His one shot, made to show her the right technique, though it does strike the target misses the bull's eye. As I was watching this episode I thought, That is how psychotherapy could best help people! It could offer them a target, and show them how to aim their energies so as to hit it.

To return to cooperative intentional communities: Their real purpose should be to help people toward actual goals, both communal and personal. Communities would be of little practical use if the members merely lived near to one another. Common goals are needed, which inspire them toward definite destinations. If their boat lacks a rudder and a compass, it will simply drift. And if no particular purpose inspires people, they may find the mere pleasure of movement sufficient for a time, but in the end they will find it tiresome.

Counseling offered with definite goals in mind might even be given a special name: "Directional Therapy." If a person takes up painting with no clear notion of what he intends to paint, he'll probably fail to achieve anything worthwhile. A direction in all things is needed.

Psychologists point out that most people are hindered by conflicting inner impulses. Those impulses arise, usually, in the subconscious, even from deep within it. Is it necessary to understand those impulses, in order to remove them? Only if they seriously impede one's ability to function. Usually it is better, however, to focus on directing positive energy than to fret over why one isn't achieving what he wants. Even a short step in the right direction can generate the needed energy for the next step.

Intentional cooperative communities provide excellent laboratories for human evolution. A shared commitment to living a better life soon shows which attitudes work well, which ones are less effective, and which ones don't work at all. If a member thinks first, "I must get my own life together, iron out my own problems, figure out what I really should be doing," he will *never* get it together! If, on the other hand, he forgets himself, and focuses on larger, objective issues; if he expands his personal needs to include the needs of others; if he determines to do something positive with his life and in company with others, he becomes an inspiration to all even when he himself is beset by serious problems in his life. Best of all, he, too, finds inspiration within himself.

An archer if he lets himself be distracted will probably miss the mark. His mind must be focused on the bull's eye. Similarly, to accomplish anything worthwhile, the mind must be withdrawn from all distractions and focused on what it wants to achieve. Distractions, in this case, include any conflicts in the subconscious.

The problem of how to redirect one's energy brings us back to Adam Smith's appeal to self-interest. When self-interest contracts upon the ego, it leads to unhappiness, and for this reason is unwholesome. When self-interest expands outward to include other interests, however, and toward working with others and helping them, it brings one happiness, inwardly, and also outwardly to everyone with whom one is in contact.

What a psychiatrist might do in practicing directional therapy is offer goals that uplift. As things are at present, while Freud's influence still hovers over the scene like a dark cloud, a patient, upon finishing his treatment, is usually sent out with the bland assurance that he is just as normal as other people—that is to say, no more neurotic than they. And what are the norms he is so confidently asked to embrace? Many, alas! are not elevating. They include selfish ambition; unappeasable desires; self-preoccupation; intolerance of ideas that don't seem familiar; anger toward anyone whose interests conflict with one's own; and emotional release such as outbursts of anger, rather than simple acceptance of objective reality. "Norms" like these, once accepted, produce a yawning sense of ennui! For any patient who hopes to find happiness in release, and certainly for any intentional community to justify its existence, the norm, instead, should be aspiration toward goals that include a true sense of inner fulfillment.

Freud's only "firm" reality was what he called the "unconscious": not so very firm, obviously—in fact, so vague as to invite almost any understanding of it one likes. His definition of it was sexual desire. Adler defined it as giving rise to the inferiority complex and the will to power. Jung defined it as the "collective unconscious." All three men taught their patients to ponder things they could neither see nor understand. Incomprehension caused them to focus on that mere shade all the more intensely.

Years ago, I was invited to lecture to a Jungian community in Germany. I felt a certain concern for them, for they seemed desperately in earnest in their desire for self-improvement. "Relax," I urged them. "Concentrate more on what you'd really like to accomplish in yourselves."

They took stern issue with me. "First," they protested, "we must free ourselves from our darknesses. We must bring them out into the open and face them honestly!"

"I agree," I said. "Self-honesty is essential. But will you really find freedom from your problems by dwelling on them so intently? To banish darkness, why not simply turn on the light?"

They continued to argue. I realized it would take

more than a lecture to change their mental conditioning. In the end their leader remonstrated with me, "My dear sir, you are just too reasonable!" Their problem was, they were committed to a philosophy that offered them no solutions: only processes.

What do I suggest as a solution? I don't say to become a "Super Achiever"! That, as we all know, is the way to an early heart attack. But what about trying to explore your own *inner* potential? That potential, while not "unconscious," may possess a degree of consciousness that is as yet unknown to you. Certainly, it is not something vague. If it seems so to anyone, then so also is genius. And if even one human being can achieve genius, all human beings can achieve it.

There are goals that all dream of, and cherish. Among them are happiness, peace of mind, inner freedom, a sense of kinship with others and with all life, and wise, sympathetic understanding. These would make a good beginning in any attempt at self-development. In addition there may be other goals, particular to each person. The important thing is that awareness expand, not contract in petty self-absorption.

In the next chapter we'll consider the question of how members of a community that is dedicated to high ideals might achieve ideals like these more easily than they could on their own. Can a goal as imprecise as happiness, for example, inspire one to action? Not as a concrete goal, admittedly. Happiness is a direction, not an end. That is to say, if one doesn't include others in his understanding of it, and share his own happiness with them, the very fulfillment he finds in it will be illusory. Gradually it will contract; eventually it will wither and die.

Happiness is not a possession: It is a state of mind, unrelated to anything material. As gas expands, so also, it may be said, does consciousness if it isn't forced into a little vessel of selfishness. Consciousness, obviously, is inconceivably subtler than gas. Thus, it may be capable of indefinite expansion. It is absurd, indeed, to think of consciousness as contained within the narrow confines of the human skull. We reach out to the world around us not only in our thoughts, but in our very consciousness, in the relationship we feel with a larger reality: with places, and with other people.

Freud described the human psyche as possessing three levels, of which the first and the last—the id and the superego—are unconscious. By his definition, only the ego is conscious. His definitions are flawed, however. Even if no lower level of consciousness is able to *will* anything on its own, it can never be completely unconscious. Since ego is the sense of self, moreover, it doesn't acquire that self-awareness from other people, as Freud claimed. Self-awareness begins with the simplest of all our realities: the fact that we have a body. It continues gaining self-definition in contact with others, but the ego is innate, not imposed. This observation is convincing if we simply observe a newborn baby with its need to concentrate on its body. This it does from the very first breath it takes. Since basic needs of this sort relate to purely physical functions, ego-awareness cannot be entirely absent even at the level of the id.

The superego, finally, as Freud explained it, is an alien imposition, neither superior to nor above the ego, but remote from and even hostile to it.

The dark realms of the id which Freud described, admittedly obscure to us in our waking state, are not absent from the Ego's awareness. They are still tied to our sense of self. In all that Wagnerian drama there is personal involvement. It is we ourselves who possess even our most hidden memories; their existence is not in someone else's mind, or more vaguely in some "collective uncon-scious." They exist in ourselves.

Freud's exclusion of the id from egoic as well as from conscious awareness opened the way for Jung's pseudo-mystical concept of a "collective unconscious." Group consciousness does, of course, influence us—more so than most people realize. Under the influence of mass emotion, rational people will sometimes behave quite irrationally. But there is nothing *un*conscious in the process. Mass influence may be regretted, when calmness returns, but to label it unconscious is only an excuse for refusing to accept all blame.

Thoughts leave an imprint on places as well. I have noted, in a lifetime of traveling, that earlier cultures, even though no longer an obvious influence on the present era, do exert a subtle one. In North America, descendants of people of foreign origin often have a rapport with the so-called American Indians* that more recent arrivals don't experience. Descendants of settlers in Australia describe themselves as feeling an attunement with the aborigines on that continent—an attunement which I, as a visitor, am less able to share. Whatever the explanation for these influences, there does seem to be a "collective" awareness of some kind which, in its awareness (not in its unconsciousness), affects us in certain ways constantly.

So then, we have an id; good. We have an ego: obvious—though the ego seems innate rather than imposed from without. What about Freud's superego? He explained it as an imposition from outside, and defined it as our "conscience." If it is imposed, the superego must not be conscience as we know it from tradition, though society's opinions do affect us, certainly. This influence, however, may be called a "social conscience"; it isn't one's deeper inner feeling of right and wrong that arises from within, and is basic to our nature. If, for example, we eat

---

*I can't resist sharing a joke here that I heard recently. Someone asked a Hopi Indian, "Would you rather be called an Indian, or a Native American?" The other replied, "Well, since we're neither, we're just glad that Columbus in discovering America wasn't looking for Turkey."

food that in some way offends against the way our bodies were made, we suffer in spite of any assurance from others that it will do us good. We know when we've offended against our bodies, for we suffer unfortunate consequences. Again if we hurt a friend, we feel badly for having done so; that feeling isn't due to any fear of other people's displeasure. It is due simply to a disharmony we've created in ourselves.* We've acted in contradiction to the natural outward flow of our heart's feelings.

In any case, the "conscience" described by Freud also works on the subconscious, and results often in repression. It is not unconscious, therefore. Freud might have designated it, instead, the Extra-ego, not the superego, for its influence comes from outside ourselves. There is a need, for all that, to recognize the existence, in addition, of a *transcendental* awareness. This awareness might be better named, the *Superconscious.* Perhaps there exists, in the unused portion of our brains, what scientists have described as our own greater potential.

Perhaps, again, the brilliance of genius is due not only to a brain of exceptional efficiency, but to the fact that the mind is open to inspiration. Perhaps even Jung's reservoir of "collective unconsciousness" exists—not unconscious, but even *more* conscious than man's usual state.

---

*Notice how people, after making an unkind remark about someone, tend to follow the remark with a light laugh. They are affirming almost reflexively an inner harmony they tell themselves has not been disturbed!

For decades, science debated whether light is a particle or a wave. The dispute was settled finally by the discovery that it is both! Perhaps that part of people's consciousness which they associate with the brain (in this analogy, the particle of light), and that which comes from a limitless source (the wave of light), will be discovered also as one and the same thing.

Many persons of genius have explained inspiration as something that comes to them in a flash. They don't work their way to it laboriously. On the other hand, the products of careful ratiocination show little evidence of having been inspired. A higher order of inspiration comes when the mind is calm and, as it were, inwardly listening. Hard work is usually needed after that, to express the inspiration to others effectively, but the inspiration itself comes with receptivity. And the conviction that comes with it is not a reasoned conclusion, even in the discovery process of scientists. In this intense awareness, the mind is calm and focused, not restless and diffused. The ego, moreover, is only minimally involved.

To clarify these ideas, visualize a stained glass window, each pane a different color. It is early in the morning, and the sun has not yet risen. The light outdoors is dim. The window's colors may be indistinguishable from one another: the reds appear like the oranges; the blues, like the greens.

Then the sun rises, and those colors each

acquire a light and beauty that seem almost their own.

To continue this image, the sun is now shining overhead; we go out to enjoy its warmth. No longer do we see the light filtered through colored glass: It is all around us, and in the blue sky above all. Indoors, the colored panes separated the light into many colors. Now it is the earth's atmosphere that gives the light its color. If there were no atmosphere around us, we would see only the sun suspended in the blackness of infinite space.

Because the human mind is limited, we like to see the sunlight diffused, rather than blazing solitarily in empty space, or framed in the panes of a stained glass window. Perhaps our brains, too, are only filters for consciousness, which the brain particularizes and frames rather than acting merely as an organ to excrete consciousness. In that case, Leonardo da Vinci might be described as the *filter* through which inspiration came to him and enabled him to produce his great art. Perhaps a wave of consciousness inspired him similarly to the way waves of light may be said to produce particles. I'm aware that this is somewhat fanciful, since light waves and light particles may prove to be co-existent. I believe, however, that I could make a good case for this analogy, if the attempt didn't demand an unwarranted detour from our argument. The wave of inspiration particularized by Leonardo may have been filtered and framed also, but differently, by other minds. His genius lay not only in his openness to receiving inspiration, but in his talent for individualizing what he'd received. It is right and natural that we honor Leonardo, the artist through whom great wonders came into being. To return, however, to the analogy of light as both a particle and a wave, if consciousness is a broader reality than that which exists in the brain, then Leonardo may be described as the *co-creator* of his works, not their originator. Leonardo was—to change the analogy—a 1,000-watt light bulb among bulbs of lower wattage, all of which receive the same electric voltage.

Many scientific discoveries have been made by more than one person at a time. This known fact suggests that the truths revealed by science may have been simply awaiting discovery by minds that were attuned to them. Indeed, it has many times been said that if Darwin had delayed the publication of *The Origin of Species* by only two weeks, Alfred Russel Wallace, who was on the same track, would be known today as the originator of the Theory of Evolution.

Nikolai Lobachevsky, in Russia, and János Bolyai, in Hungary, discovered non-Euclidian geometry more or less simultaneously. Euclid's geometry had been the unchallenged authority for more than two thousand years. All at once these two men, unknown to one another, made the same revolutionary breakthrough.

In mathematics, again, Isaac Newton in England and Baron Leibniz in Germany (he who first drew attention to the subconscious) discovered calculus. They weren't collaborators, but their discovery came almost together.

Consider, too, the waves of artistic inspiration that move across countries and cultures. They touched Germany during the eighteenth and nineteenth centuries, when great masterpieces of music were produced; Athens, Greece, during the fourth century B.C., with the flowering of great philosophy; France in the seventeenth century, inspiring the great plays of Corneille, Racine, and Molière.

In studying this historical phenomenon, case after case presents itself in support of the theory that consciousness is not a creation of the brain, but is supplied to the brain, rather, giving it its very power to think.

To return to Carl Jung's "collective unconscious": If his reference was not to something literally unconscious; if it wasn't a mere composite of many people's thoughts, but rather a source from which their thoughts derive: what can it be? The world's cultures, in this case, must have developed not only from collective decisions, but from attunement with larger aspects of consciousness itself. Scientific invention, artistic inspiration, literary inspiration, great mental achievements of all kinds: all these come from attunement with various levels of consciousness, and not from thinking, thinking,

thinking while the mind, like a whirling dervish, grows dizzy with so much effort.

I have suggested that this greater consciousness be called the *superconscious*. Freud's appellation, the superego, is misleading. He related it to the superficial "conscience" which society, parents, religion, and other authority figures impose upon us. He said their strictures are responsible for the conflicts people experience between the superego and the nature they were born with—the id, or aggregate of "animal" impulses. Conscience, as Freud defined it, is the cause of most people's unhappiness, for their response to its strictures often makes them suppress what they really want in order to adjust their behavior to others' demands.

Inner conflict, in this view, is inevitable. It forces the repression of our natural impulses, and causes inner tension and frustration. In extreme cases, it can lead to madness. Human life, therefore, can never transcend the level of mere compromise—a Hegelian synthesis between two harsh alternatives: personal self-interest on the one hand; society's self-interest on the other. Happiness is not possible, and the best we may hope for is, by releasing our repressions, to function somewhat normally in a basically abnormal world where conflict and competition are the only "norms." Suppression is the "Trojan horse within the walls" that threatens our peace of mind. Release from suppression is, Freud insisted, the only possible way to fulfillment.

Once again, however, we must pose the simple question: *Does it work?*

There is an aspect of suppression that too few people, especially since Freud, have taken sufficiently into account. It is that suppression may sometimes actually be a good thing—not because it helps us to avoid shame and ignominy, but because it helps us to develop inner strength and nobility of character. These are assets, and enrich the soil in which the tree of happiness grows.

Imagine a fairly common situation: A man loves a woman, and she requites his love. She poses a threat, however, to some principle that he holds dear. Perhaps that principle is his love of country, or of a noble cause, or of God. Perhaps, in the first alternative, the woman belongs to an enemy nation. Perhaps, in the second, she isn't interested in his cause. Perhaps, in the third, she is wholly committed to worldly pursuits and indifferent to his spiritual aspirations. What ought he to do?

In each case, a psychoanalyst might say to him, "Your conscience has been imposed upon you by society. It has no objective validity. Do, therefore, what feels good to you. If, in choosing the path of honor (as you call it), you renounce love, you will only suffer, for you'll have repressed your real desire. What point is there in suffering? Accept the fact that fulfilling the desire is, in your case, the *only* good. Choose the girl."

Let us assume the man accepts this advice. In

his heart, however, he knows he is losing something precious. For a time, he might be happy with his choice. Eventually, however, he will certainly suffer. For by denying his ideals he will deaden a very real part of himself.

To renounce personal gratification for a principle is, according to many psychoanalysts, a mistake often made. In every culture, however, renunciation of this sort is considered a virtue and a pathway to honor. Pain is not always a bad thing. To do what one feels to be *right,* not merely pleasant, is the way to true and lasting happiness. Though this uphill path is not always enjoyable, its rewards are greater than the consolation one experiences in any mere wave of emotion. Self-control, like a river, leads to a calm sea. Was Freud right? Has humanity for so many centuries been wrong?

"Do what feels good," the psychiatrist may say. Does it "feel good," then, to affirm selfishness? We have seen that, in the long run, it does not. The way to "feel good" is to expand your self-identity, not to contract it.

Some years ago I read an account of a woman whose husband had died recently. Someone asked a friend of hers how she was doing. "Oh, *marvelously!*" replied the friend. "She's kept on such heavy sedation that she hardly knows what she's missing." Is it really good to place so high a priority on avoiding pain? When pain is faced and accepted, it can produce an increase of insight. To seek always to avoid pain is a sign of emotional immaturity. It indicates a refusal to face reality.

Blocked energy doesn't shrivel up and die, but if it is *redirected* it can generate great power. Pain encourages us to re-think our priorities. If suppressed energy is released and channeled wisely, initial disappointments may lead to increasing success and happiness.

Genius would never flourish if it compromised weakly with every social convention. Neither would heroism. True conscience, as opposed to the superficial "conscience" which Freud connected with the superego, summons us to live up to the highest that is in us. This conscience comes from within ourselves; it is never imposed from without. This is a more difficult path, granted, than lying on a couch and giving utterance to a stream of consciousness in the hope of releasing blocked energy. In the end, however, it is infinitely more rewarding.

One means of achieving the rewards of self-conquest may be found in communities. For *outer* goals are needed too, towards which people can aspire *together.* If intentional communities were only a matter of each member exploring his own potentials, the best solution might be to become a hermit. But people need other people. Company and environment are important, and exert on us all a powerful influence. Communities that are dedicated to high principles can inspire members to make an effort that many of them might never succeed in making on their own.

In the next, and last, chapter we shall consider what, specifically, a community might do to establish goals that are expansive, rather than merely narrow and contractive.

CHAPTER TEN

❋

Conscious Evolution and the Small Communities Solution

Self-expansion and aspiration are among life's basic impulses. Self-expansion one sees everywhere, as living forms burst out of their seeds and grow to maturity. We mentioned this process when referring to the expanding rings in a tree trunk. Aspiration, again, is expressed physically in plants as they reach toward the sun. These two impulses are even more evident in the expansion and aspiration of consciousness, especially after evolution reaches the human stage. Self-expansion is seen from the beginning of life in the desire to know and to experience. It is seen in love for one's fellow creatures. It is seen in the upward thrust of evolution toward greater awareness. It is seen also in artists, in their hope of creating works of inspiration.

These assertions may cause skeptics to scoff at what they consider "mere flights of poetic sentiment." Mechanisms, to them, are what it's all about, whether in biology and physics or in economics and politics. It is, however, this very preoccupation with the mechanics of things, to the exclusion of the conscious purpose that every creature expresses, which stands in urgent need of correction. Otherwise, cynicism may plunge the human race into a darkness from which it may not easily re-emerge.

Everything can be explained in terms of whatever point of view one selects. Who can say that the physicist understands reality better than the poet? The physicist understands with the mind; the poet, with the heart. Both of these, expressing reason and feeling, are part of reality. And both are, in the kaleidoscope of vast possibilities, infinite. As the atom is the key to the universe, and the ego the key to all humanity, so *any* starting point can be taken as the key to everything. The poet Keats grieved, "There was an awful rainbow once in heaven. . . . She is given in the dull catalogue of common things." Yet why should the beauty of a rainbow not be accepted even today as belonging to its intrinsic reality?

The modern mechanistic outlook has brought us blindfolded to the brink of disaster, for the mechanics of destruction are matched by the growing belief (a mere jiggle of that kaleidoscope!) that nothing means anything anyway. Moral and spiritual values have given precedence to fascination with mechanisms and gadgetry.

Today's great need is for increased moral sensitivity, and a halt to the modish denigration of all moral values. "Value judgments" are decried in university classes as being contrary to the proved truth, "All is relative." Forgotten in those numbing classroom discussions is the simple fact that the word "relativity" implies *relationships.* I made this case at length in my book, *Out of the Labyrinth,* where I pointed out that moral values, though not absolute (since all is relative), are yet directional in their relativity, and in that sense are universal. Their roots lie in human nature, of which certain realities never change. What an adult eats would be harmful to a newborn baby. The rules of life change with the maturing of wisdom, but they apply equally to all who are at the same stage of development.

One of the most appalling photographs I've ever seen was of a group of cannibals gloating around a human corpse as they prepared to eat it. Obviously it seemed to them, at their level of understanding, that they were doing a wonderful thing. Civilized people, similarly, might rub their hands together in happy anticipation before a banquet. The facial expressions of those cannibals, however, were bestial, devoid of anything you and I would think of as normal human feeling. "Who are we," do you say, "to impose our own value judgments on them?" The answer is obvious: Those savages were already self-judged. The glee they showed in their depravity revealed as much pain as pleasure. Their very enjoyment in that act would certainly disgust them someday, when their sensitivity became more refined. In terms of what every human being really wants—pure happiness, for example, and inner peace—their "delight" was clearly gross and brutish, not elevated.

To choose another much more banal example: Isn't there a certain pleasure in scratching a mosquito bite? But doesn't it at the same time hurt to scratch it? The prurience of some pleasures is also painful. That is why sense orgies are so often followed by disgust. People who make pleasure their main goal in life show no happiness in their eyes. What they reveal, rather, is minds that are dull and restless, and feelings that can no longer delight in anything except wallowing, like buffaloes, in the "primal mud."

Whatever reality we see around us is what we ourselves are capable of seeing. Everything reflects back to us who and what we are. If we choose with economists to define wealth solely in terms of money and property, then that, for us, is all that wealth is. If we choose to see evolution only in terms of survival, then that, again (for us at least) is what evolution is all about. And if we choose to define humanity by its "animal" nature, then that again—for us; not necessarily for others!—is all it is. Someone who had been trained in modern science once said to me matter-of-factly, "We are all just animals." I replied, "Speak for yourself!" One who looks for the animal in man may not respect a Buddha. Even depraved human beings, however, can be seen with eyes of kindness and respect, and with a view to their potential greatness. If we prefer to see them in terms of that latent perfection, we not only may inspire them to work toward it, but inspire ourselves, too, toward that end.

Excessive concentration on mechanisms leaves no space for genius, or wisdom, or inspiration, which appear repeatedly in the course of history. On the other hand, to view life in terms of upward movement, of self-expansion and aspiration, is to bring to ourselves the fulfillment everyone, whether consciously or not, is seeking.

We have seen in these chapters that humanity, far from being diminished by the discoveries of astronomy, has achieved a more central place in the universe than it knew when people believed the universe was geocentric. "Center everywhere, circumference nowhere": the cosmology of wisdom. In the universe that science has shown us, every atom—and by extension every ego—may legitimately be considered central to everything. Fully to understand the one is, to that degree, to understand all.

We speak here, however, especially of centers of consciousness. Solutions to the problems addressed in this book must not be sought in some new theory but in direct, conscious experience. They must be sought not in grand reforming schemes, but on a small scale, where it may still be possible to make alterations. If a new idea is found to work well, and if it fills a universal need, it will naturally spread.

Sweeping social reforms never really change anything. If they don't have people's willing consent, they will be circumvented at every opportunity. The French have a saying that applies well to such overzealous reforms: *"Plus ça change, plus c'est la même chose:* The more things change, the more they remain as they always were." When the dust that was kicked up by reforming zeal has settled, and perhaps after a few million people have been slaughtered in the name of the Great Cause, nothing, really, has changed. Why not? Because human nature was not consulted.

Every reform must elicit willing cooperation from the people it affects. It must work with human nature as it is, and not try to make it what the theorists think it ought to be.

In communist Russia, only two percent of farmland was owned privately. That minute portion, however, yielded some sixty percent of the country's crops. No social edict could have altered the simple fact, which Adam Smith noted, that people will always promote their own interest. Social reforms must begin by recognizing this simple truth, and appealing to it. A new principle cannot be driven down people's throats. If they find it unpalatable, they are more likely to gag on it than plead for a second helping. Reforms must be recognized as desirable *by the people themselves.* And that recognition cannot be of the intellect only: It must also include the heart.

It is not necessary that millions of people be convinced. A few individuals only, inspired to give a new idea a try, are enough to spark a conflagration which will eventually consume the whole forest of old ways. The magnetism of those old ways lies in nothing but their inertia. A new, dynamic energy will break up that resistance, even as the warmth of spring changes an ice field into a floe that is soon swept away by a rushing river.

Many years ago there appeared in *Punch,* the English humor magazine, a cartoon depicting a crowd of people at a railway station. The cartoon was in three segments, in the first of which all the people were standing about or sitting on suitcases, waiting for something. In the second, one man was shown hurrying past them with an air of urgency. In the third, all were rushing in the same direction.

People will follow dynamic energy, if they think it in their interest to do so. In the cartoon, the people were evidently worried lest their train leave without them. Action stirs people; inert theories lull them to inaction. If even a few people commit themselves to a good idea, others will imitate them, in time. It isn't often that new movements and ideas are quickly accepted; usually, at least a generation must pass. For one thing, few people have the courage to adopt a new thing openly. They may secretly believe in it, but they fear that it may deprive them of acceptance by others. The power of tradition is too great for them. Once, however, new ground has been broken and new crops planted, if the seeds yield a bountiful harvest increasing numbers will derive benefit from what has been done. A new idea will be embraced once people have seen it in action and like what they see.

Small, intentional, cooperative communities are the ideal solution for bringing real change to the modern world. What is needed is groups of people actually *living* lives together that are sane, happy, and purposeful.

Cooperative communities are an answer to the pseudo-scientific dogma, expressed by Adam Smith, that competition is the way to success. Cooperation should be actively encouraged—internally among the members; externally with the greater society; idealistically by attunement with aspects of their own nature that uplift them; realistically, with objective and natural law; and spiritually, by cooperation with truth.

I propose *communities* because, although it is always in any case the individuals in a group who need to be inspired, only the united influence of a group of people can produce a significant impact on society. Even the founders of history's great movements such as Buddhism and Christianity needed followers to perpetuate their teachings. The communities I envision are not shadow groups huddled in basements by candlelight, hatching dark plots. They are visible, open, and reachable. And they are based not on rigid control, but on fairness and flexibility, accepting idiosyncrasy as perfectly normal in human affairs.

Repeatedly we have seen in these pages that rigid systems, though useful up to a point, obstruct further development, for they discourage creativity. Only flexibility facilitates growth, whether in individuals or in whole systems. Rigidity comes when people are afraid of making mistakes. Errors, on the other hand, if not too outrageous, should be tolerated and not condemned. People need the freedom to err, for only thus does understanding develop. Reasonable acceptance of error engenders a feeling of support and fosters, in return, a cooperative spirit.

It is too much to expect perfection in an imperfect world. One man's definition of an ideal might be another's of mediocrity. The best hope for a community lies only in striving for a good *direction:* directional improvement, directional upliftment, directional growth in understanding, directional fulfillment. In all these respects the direction can be upward. That is to say, it can take people toward ever broader vistas.

The authors we've studied in these pages dealt less with living realities than with fixed concepts. Marx envisioned communism as an end in itself:

the triumph of what might facetiously be called "mindlessness over matter." (Even matter is more adaptable than Marx was with his rigid theories!) Freud didn't offer progress *toward* anything. In fact, none of those writers did. What they focused on primarily was information. What they wanted, and what people generally seem to want in the present period of historic transition from a solid, geocentric view of the universe to a fluid view of matter as energy, is an ever-swelling tide of information. Above all what they want is to know how things work. Today they seem more fascinated than ever by this information binge, and by the technology it has produced.

"Did you know that a mere square inch of sky photographed through the Hubble telescope has revealed millions of galaxies?" "No! Well, and here's another one: Did you know that the algae on a pond may contain enough nourishment to feed the entire human race?" "Well, I'm not up on the esoterica of pond scum, but do you realize that with a simple quartz crystal, information can actually be transmitted?" And so it goes on, and on. We are so deluged with facts that it has become virtually impossible to know what to do with them all. Even more difficult is it to ponder imponderables, like consciousness.

"Has man evolved more in producing a brain," was the question asked by the psychologist James F. Crow in a statement we quoted earlier, "than the elephant has in producing a trunk?" From Crow's question it is clear that he would have spurned this book, with its insistence that human progress can be measured by the refinement of consciousness, and not by the amount of information gathered or by the number of mechanisms developed. Crow was wrong in any case, however, for that evolution is *progressive* is a fact demonstrated most clearly with the appearance of *homo sapiens.* But of course his argument was based on the premise of purely physical changes. Moreover, his alternatives are unreasonable, for the human brain and an elephant's trunk are not even logical oppositions. Crow was merely trying, with heavy humor, to ridicule what he considered man's self-delusion in thinking himself important in the great scheme of things. Science, he believed, had shown man to be quite insignificant. (One is tempted to imagine standees at the back of Crow's lecture hall making catcalls and shouting, "Whose brain are you talking about, Jim? *Your own?* If so, my vote goes to the elephant!")

Crow would have shown himself more discerning had he phrased his question thus: "Has man evolved more in producing a brain than the porpoise, also a mammal, has in learning to live under water?" In this case the answer might be, "No, not if a worldwide flood should occur, for in that case the porpoise would survive, whereas man would not." In other words, if survival were the entire criterion of evolutional success, then human beings, despite their intelligence, might find themselves holding the loser's straw. Would humanity, in that case, deserve to be written off as a failure? By no means! The earth itself would give ample testimony to the greatness of man's achievements. In any ordinary context, intelligence, and the refinement of awareness, are what evolution is really all about.

Survival, as we have seen, is not the centerpiece Darwin thought it to be in his evolutionary display. It is merely the table on which he placed his carefully assembled items. Otherwise, the salient fact presented by his evidence is that all life demonstrates to varying degrees an *awareness* of its existence, and a self-motivated thrust toward ever-expanding awareness.

Lower forms may defy Descartes' dictum, "I think, therefore I am." Molluscs and other primitive creatures don't give the impression that they think at all. What they display are only urges. They wouldn't have even those urges, however, if they weren't conscious. Can even primitive emotions be discerned in such blind impulses? Possibly not. Nevertheless, all life forms cling to whatever degree of awareness they do have, and *consciously* resist any perceived threat to that awareness.

Beyond the mere urge to survive, there is something else all living creatures seek. To whatever degree their awareness allows, they seek to *enjoy* their existence. Since awareness is in many cases so dim that it is doubtful they actually *enjoy* anything, what might be said is that "enjoyment," for them, consists of having continued awareness as opposed to losing all awareness.

Consciousness introduces *progress* into the schema of evolution. Otherwise we'd have only change and diversity. Evolution is upward because it manifests ever-clearer awareness. Upon reaching the human level, it demonstrates an increasing attachment to, and appreciation for, personal fulfillment.

The discovery that the earth is not the center of the universe brought man the realization that he is not God's supreme achievement in the material order of things. But if man is the key to all things, then the materialism of the skeptic collapses: Life itself takes on rich meaning, and the future shines before us with new hope. No adherent of the philosophies of Machiavelli, Smith, Darwin, or Freud can do better than survive. He cannot survive *happily.*

In the last chapter I suggested that psychotherapy be conducted with specific goals in mind, the name I proposed being "Directional Therapy." The guidance that people receive in intentional cooperative communities would be given to help them in a natural direction for themselves. Modern psychiatry, too, is moving toward a similar concept. In the communities of which I have actual experience, what visitors notice first is the glow of well-being in the members' eyes. Even guests' eyes shine after a few days. Such a sense of well-being is not so often seen where people are without a sense of purpose. Small intentional cooperative communities, conscious in the way they direct their energy, can fulfill a great need in the present age, as they have repeatedly in the past.

During the time when ancient Rome was disintegrating, what kept Western civilization alive was the prevalence of monasteries. Historians agree that those communities were to a great extent responsible for maintaining the stability of society. It wasn't only that they preserved precious manuscripts from being lost or destroyed, or that they kept literacy alive—although these contributions were important. Their chief contribution was that they inspired people to a belief in higher values. In the spiritual desert that was creeping over society, when refined understanding languished, the monasteries provided little oases of hope.

The primary explanation for this phenomenon was that they offered living examples. More than that, they subtly influenced society by their uplifted consciousness. Groups of dedicated men and women, united in love for high principles, raised the general awareness. It always happens that when a Leonardo da Vinci brings his subtle inspirations into manifestation through his art; when an Isaac Newton deepens the world's understanding through his discoveries; when a George Washington, a John Adams, and a Thomas Jefferson bring deeper political insight to bear on molding a new nation, all of them bring to humanity not only those insights, but a hint of the contact they themselves have attained with higher consciousness. It was this influence, above all, that the monasteries imparted. It affected the consciousness even of people who had no great interest, personally, in questions of faith.

So far in this book I have touched only lightly on the direct influence of consciousness as opposed to the indirect effect produced on the mind by new discoveries, insights, and inspirations. Consciousness is not confined in the brain, but includes *super*conscious levels of awareness. Human beings who successfully raise their awareness to those levels, and who then give outward expression to their deepened insights, render the greatest possible service to mankind by bringing that contact *down* to levels where people can actually *feel* those realities. An inspired piece of music, for example, thrills the hearts of its listeners, and puts them in contact with levels of understanding which they might otherwise have not even imagined existed.

The monasteries, similarly, in the uplifted consciousness of their monks and nuns, had a transforming influence that extended far beyond their walls, greatly exceeding the influence of their personal example. The very atmosphere around them was uplifting. Because they were united in one thought form, the power of their thought was magnified both for themselves and for those out "in the world."

In the communities I propose, there is no need, today, for large, central organizations to sustain them. It is possible for individuals, and certainly for groups, to support themselves far away from the big cities and without the usual alternatives for country dwellers, such as farming. With telephones, computers, e-mail, and fax machines, self-support is feasible for everyone, even from places that are otherwise isolated.

What the monasteries generated during the Dark Ages was, above all, a renewal of *spiritual faith.* Could cooperative communities today be successful *without* that spiritual element? In most attempts at social upliftment, spirituality has been almost conscientiously ignored. The disinterest has been due partly to a fear of being sucked down by theological quicksands or embroiled in sectarian bickering. It has been due partly, also, to the aridity of society's bias in favor of mechanisms. If, however, we ask again the question posed before, "Does it work?" we see that in general those attempts have been disappointing. They lacked the one ingredient essential to human upliftment: inspiration. Instead, what they've offered is a convenient but pale compromise between the desire to do good and the inability to imagine anything more interesting than a sappy definition of that "good." There they all were, those willing workers, recommending as "norms" of behavior what they themselves had long ago rejected in their desire to "serve" others! Their very dedication was, for them personally, a travesty.

I remember a cousin of mine writing to me while both of us were in college—she at Wellesley, I at Brown University—to say that she'd been thinking of becoming a medical doctor. "I certainly approve of that ambition," I wrote back. "Medicine is a noble profession. And yet, you've obliged me to think more particularly about my own life. I also, as you know, want to help others. Yet what I'd like to offer them is more than the 'norm' of being well again. I'd like in some way to inspire 'normal' people to become better."

Can cooperative communities thrive without a base in spirituality? Is it even possible for consciousness to evolve upward, if there are no spiritual ideals? It was this *consciousness* in the monasteries that inspired people everywhere, not only their renunciation of worldly pleasures, which was itself negative. What inspired others was their love for God. Has any merely social ideal ever had so profound an effect? None that I'm aware of. In fact, I very much doubt whether any cooperative community could succeed if it lacked a spiritual focus. Attempts to do so seem always to have been "one-horsepower," lackluster affairs.

I distinguish between spirituality and religion.

To me, spirituality means an expansion of sympathy, without the necessity for such tags as "Christian sympathy" or "Jewish sympathy" or "Buddhist" or "Hindu" sympathy. It means to care about others without necessarily specifying that one's care is in the name of some religion. It means to have ideals that inspire one to soar in consciousness. A person needn't belong to any specific religion, nor hold any specifically religious beliefs. An atheist, in this sense, would be rendering a spiritual service if he brought relief to others in pain. And an ardent religious believer would display a want of spirituality if he denied such relief to "non-believers," as was known to happen, for example, among missionaries in India. Truth never marches with a flag. Religious institutions misrepresent themselves if, buttressed by their creeds and dogmas, they pose as guard towers of spirituality.

Religious institutions were of course created to promote spiritual truths. All too many, however, diluted their initial inspiration in time by an excessive focus on institutionalism without sufficient devotion to the practice of their ideals. Without actual practice, sincerity is lost, and people end up paying mere lip service to the ideals they profess. Many people in the name of religion act as if the whole point of all their bustling were only to "get the word out." Thus, although religious institutions do good in bringing spiritual truths to people's awareness, often they dilute those principles by pretending to have a monopoly on them, even to the point of claiming that, to be "saved," one must sign up as a member.

When anyone asks me, "To what faith do you belong?" I reply, "Isn't it enough that one *have* faith?" If pressed further I explain, "I am universal. That is to say, I'm not any kind of 'ist.' I simply believe in what I've experienced. In that spirit I'm a Christian, Jew, Hindu, Buddhist, Muslim—in fact, as I say, I'm universal. The important thing to me is the truth underlying all those 'isms.'"

Human nature, unfortunately, is not comfortable without labels to paste onto its ideas. What I'd like to say, therefore, is simply that spirituality means *living* one's aspirations, not defining them with exquisite exactitude. We should aspire toward an ever-higher, more expansive consciousness, and not try to win smiles of approval from mitred dignitaries. Whatever our ideals, spirituality should be, for each of us, a continual refining of consciousness.

If such be the case, where does God fit into the picture? Ought people, as individuals and as communities, to believe in a Supreme Being? *"Ought"* is a loaded word! There is no obligation in sincerity. The word "God" is only a symbol. What we "ought" to do, rather, is find what we can believe in sincerely.

All of us believe in life; even Darwin gave us that much. It is our belief in life that forms the actual basis for any faith we have.

We believe in the plain fact that we are conscious of existing: This is our one certainty. We also know we'd rather enjoy this consciousness than loathe it. Having granted that much, we may safely add that we would rather increase that enjoyment than diminish it, and that this preference is dynamic, not static.

The trouble with most definitions of God is that they are static. To "believe" in a definition is to substitute an inert symbol for what all of us really want and believe in: an increase of conscious joy. We don't want life to be like a stagnant pond: We want it flowing like a stream. It can interest none of us to believe in something we don't even consider our own business. When people's feelings rise to embrace a concept, it is the intensity of their feeling that constitutes their belief, not the object itself.

Few people really know what they're saying when they claim to believe in God. What they really mean is that they believe in their aspiration, their *direction of energy* toward something higher than their present state.

People need symbols as incentives. Their faith, however, is defined by the inner direction taken by their consciousness. "God," as far as human understanding is concerned, is a symbol, but the word symbolizes for the mind an upward aspiration toward some perfection yet to be realized. There are attitudes that inspire all of us: kindness, for example, and compassion. There are also other attitudes that depress us, such as resentment and doubt. God symbolizes a goal toward which we can rise. Satan, on the other hand, symbolizes the ever-present appeal of depressive energy. Both directions are principles, and as such are constant. Human feelings, by contrast, are inconstant. We see a glorious sunset, and our hearts rise joyfully in recognition of its beauty. The next day, the sunset may be just as beautiful, but our thoughts are distracted; we are not moved by it. The question is, Was it the sunset that gave us joy? Or did we give *ourselves* joy, by the way we reacted to it?*

The next question, then, is, Do we *create* God by our belief in him? We may thank him for giving us the child we always wanted, but was it really his gift? And would our belief in him be as deep if the child died? Voltaire said, "If God didn't exist, it would be necessary to invent him." Is God's existence something we've invented, out of merely human necessity? Maybe the birth and death of that child were only accidents.

God is a concept, and concepts are mental impositions on reality. They are an attempt to make sense out of what might otherwise seem only random occurrences. Every concept, however, loses meaning for us the more we try to define it exactly. The only value in the word "God" is that it symbolizes for us something toward which we all,

---

*There are other related questions: for instance, if there are no clouds in the sky one evening, but our minds are tranquil, may we not feel the same joy we did as in watching a beautiful sunset?

consciously or unconsciously, aspire. Whether or not we believe in God is less important than what we *are,* ourselves.

Let us consider once again a phenomenon we touched on in the last chapter: *genius.* Is genius produced in the mind? or is it the result of inspirations *received by* the mind? Inspiration, the secret of true genius, comes when the mind is prepared to receive it. It cannot be whipped up artificially.

Devotion to God, then, and sincerity of belief in him, is a two-way street. Our belief is generated by our own thoughts, but it also becomes, increasingly, a response to something we actually receive in holding that thought. Belief uplifts the mind, and opens it in an attitude of "listening." As in the case of genius, if something really *is* "up there" that can uplift us, our receptivity alone is what can make it manifest.

Artistic works that are mind-born lack inspiration; they may even be described as stillborn. There is a greater consciousness, however, of which human mentation is only a part. How we draw on that consciousness is determined by how we open ourselves to it. Do we create it, perhaps, by our very expectations?

Here lies the secret that tips the scale in favor of an existing, conscious, and universal reality: The less we emphasize ourselves, the more clear our insight into that uplifted consciousness becomes. We cannot receive truly lofty inspirations as long as we busy ourselves thinking. The more we can still our thoughts, however, the clearer the insights we receive. In other words, the very effort to "create" God is a sure way of losing him! The more we concentrate on actual experience, moreover, instead of trying to define experience, the more we develop real faith. Belief is a projection. Faith is a living experience.

I remember a discussion I had many years ago with a teenage boy. We were in a group that was singing folk music. He told me that he was an atheist.

"I wonder if you really are," I said. "You may not accept any definition of God you've ever heard: a divine Personage, for example, who commands people to do this and not do that, and who punishes them if they disobey. You may not even accept that it is possible for intelligence to exist without a physical brain. Even so, will you tell me there isn't *something* in life that you consider worth striving toward? And isn't that at least a start toward thinking there may be some higher reality than your own?" My argument made no impression on him. God, he persisted, simply doesn't exist. I dropped the subject, and we went back to singing.

Later on I was driving him and two other singers to their homes. A girl who was with us, about sixteen years of age, announced cynically, "I don't believe in love. It just doesn't exist!" I thought, She's no doubt suffered some disappointment in love. Will she have the same thought two months from now?

Anyway, after I'd left her at her home the boy turned to me in amazement and exclaimed, "Can you imagine that? not believing in *love!*"

With a smile I replied, "And you call yourself an atheist?"

If he thought people should believe in love, what could his meaning be except that love, by his understanding, is a reality? Love in that case, like consciousness, cannot be a mere creation of the brain. Were it such, it would be impossible to share the experience of it with anyone else. The word "love" wouldn't even exist. But love, as this young man understood, is a universal fact.

In Australia many years ago a man said to me, "I'm an atheist. If you believe in God, can you define him in such a way as to mean something to me?"

I thought for a moment, then answered, "Would it help you to think of God as the highest potential you can imagine for yourself?"

He was taken aback. "Well, ye-e-es," he replied slowly, "Yeah, sure, I can live with that!"

What is sincere aspiration toward any higher consciousness than our own, if not spiritual? Labels don't matter. The important thing is that our direction of aspiration be *upward.*

Upward aspiration is a desperate need in the

modern age. Too many concepts have been tossed at us. What we need is *experience*—the experience of love, for example—not the concept of it. If we pride ourselves on our "hard-headed realism," we shouldn't dismiss higher possibilities without even a test.

We need ideals that can be defined in terms of the possible. (I like to think of myself as a devotee of the possible.) We need to understand upward evolution in terms of a fulfillment everyone wants who has any real hope in life. To have no higher aim than pleasure and self-aggrandizement is to abandon oneself to a meaningless existence. In that case, it would be pointless to create *intentional* communities, for a community that had no uplifting aim would be a lackluster affair, doomed to an early demise.

Well, but must those aims be *spiritual?* The truth is, any other definition brings us back to contractive self-interest, an affirmation of ego-consciousness, and the death of all wisdom. Inevitably there follows a diminishing of awareness. We have seen even in works of art that greatness increases in *inverse proportion* to the degree of ego-consciousness they express. To be free inwardly means far more than mere release from subconscious repressions. It means, above all, emerging from the abyss of self-absorption. Inner freedom expands in *direct* proportion to how fully we embrace greater realities.

In cooperative communities, experience has demonstrated repeatedly that the less one's self-preoccupation, the greater one's happiness. Happiness is not a condition to be *attained* so much as a reality already existent within oneself, a state of consciousness that is revealed, like the sunlight when the clouds obscuring it have been removed.

Human evolution has not been of a physical nature since *homo sapiens* first appeared on this planet. Since then, our evolution has been a matter largely of refining our consciousness. Consciousness, however, can be taken in many directions, by no means all of them *upward*. For once evolution reaches the human level, upward movement ceases to be an instinctive urge. Human intelligence can alter that course, or increase its upward impetus. It can make life's course as hilly or as winding as it chooses. It can even justify, with its talent for twisting reason, a downward direction.

To work at improving oneself is better, obviously, than correcting others while doing nothing to correct oneself. Self-improvement, however, is not easy among people whose first impulse, often, is to correct or blame others. Negativity has its own power to influence. Encouragement toward self-development, on the other hand, is natural in cooperative communities, whose very reason for existence is self-perfection.

Communities, as I indicated earlier, can be wonderful laboratories of self-discovery. To set aside what *you* want, to choose instead what is best for everyone—and above all, to choose what is right—

such discernment is more easily developed in a cooperative community than in the company of self-interested people. Such is the benefit of living in a cooperative, intentional community as opposed to living where expressions of kindness are often trampled upon in the stampede for self-aggrandizement.

To preserve a sense of humor in the face of vicissitudes, again, is desirable. Humor, however, is often misunderstood in the marketplace. Forgiveness is often embarrassing for those who harbor resentments. Intentional communities encourage their members to develop such attitudes.

Consider an example of a couple in a cooperative community who lost their home in a forest fire. The wife had given birth ten days previously to their first child. The loss was almost more than she could bear. Her husband, desiring to console her, smiled and said with tender humor, "Well, at least we won't have any more worries about those leaks we were having in the roof!" Exceptional people elsewhere might have reacted with similar courage, but in a cooperative community his statement had the additional implication, "What are we *really* doing with our lives? Isn't there something far more worthwhile that we're living for?"

To think of others' needs first, rather than of one's own, is, again, more easily generated in a cooperative community than in places where people oppose generosity with the slogan, "Look out for number one!" Indeed, if a community has a truly expansive outlook, it will embrace the larger community also in its concerns, instead of focusing only on its own needs.

It was because of attitudes like these that the monasteries during the Dark Ages were so forceful a presence. One reads about how the monks and nuns inspired others. An individual may be able to exert a positive influence on his own, but unless his energy is combined with that of others he will be likely to draw attention to himself as a unique person, rather than inspire others to think that they too might be able to develop his qualities themselves.

All human beings can develop nobility of nature. They can be happy, even when confronted by great adversity; friendly, even to those who hate them; more concerned for what is right than with anything they might, personally, prefer; willing to place others' needs before their own. For most people, however, such attitudes go against the grain of deep habit. Seldom, if ever, do attitudes like these come easily. The example of others is usually needed to inspire such attitudes in oneself. Under such an influence, those attitudes can gradually become second nature.

A few deeply committed individuals, in whom such attitudes have developed over years of practice, can inspire countless others. Hence the importance not only of communities, but also of good leaders.

A good leader asks more of himself than he does

of anyone else. He puts his own needs last, not first. Because of his dedication to truth, he works with willing disinterest for the welfare of all. He asks nothing of others that he is not willing to do, personally. He sets the first example of right attitudes, and never thinks, "What's in it for me?" or, "What's in it for our community?" Always, his first concern is, "What is right and true?"

In those early monasteries, what accounted for their selflessness was above all their faith in God. Indeed, they had more than faith: They had heartfelt *love* for God. Can we expect to develop such a spirit in today's world? Without love, certainly, the balloon of aspiration will never rise high off the ground.

Many people, myself included, object to being told what they should believe. I particularly resist people's clumsy attempts to convert me. Yet I do like to share with others my enthusiasms: something beautiful, perhaps, or meaningful, or true.

If I see a colorful field of tulips, I want to tell everyone, "Do go see that field if you can! It will inspire you." In what way would this sharing differ from the tactics of conversion I deplore? Perhaps the difference can be explained thus: When I find something beautiful, I don't beg people to go see it as though my own peace of mind depended on their going. No strings are attached to my suggestion. Again, I don't urge people to see those tulips with a view to promoting something else, as advertisements do, and as religious people do when, though seeming to praise something else, their real aim is to promote their own beliefs. Beauty is not something one can possess; it is impersonal and abstract, like truth or the laws of science. Can anyone *own* the Law of Gravity? Not even Isaac Newton, its discoverer, could possess it.

For this reason also I don't feel to name here the communities of which I am the founder. It isn't that I'm shy to speak about them. Indeed, if anything I've done deserves to be so called, they are my crowning achievement. What I'm proposing here, however, is a concept, not a place. I've learned, moreover, that people often prefer sound theories to even sounder accomplishments. Very well then, think of this book as the proposal of a theory, and forget the specifics. My only wish is that you take these concepts seriously.

These ideas are like seeds: They can grow and spread, in time to become a forest of many types of communities. Cooperative communities are too universal a need in this age for any limited vision of them. No specific type of community will fill that need. What I'm offering here is a solution that has been tested and proved—not once only, but many times throughout the ages. Yes, the idea works.

Take this hypothetical example: Supposing a cooperative community has inspired a few people to live serene, happy, and successful lives. Then suppose they separate, and move to different cities.

Would their example have the same impact on others as it did while they lived together? Imagine them working in busy offices and commuting from ordinary suburbs. Those they meet might benefit from their example of serenity and happiness, and appreciate the atmosphere of peace they emanate. Would their example, however, have a *practical* impact on other lives? People might conclude from meeting them that they are very special, but not "normal" like themselves. Few, if any, would even think of emulating the example of such people. Gathered together in a community, however, and dedicated with others to a high ideal, their example will more likely become contagious. Others might soon decide that what makes them so special is something they, too, could do in their own lives.

In the Dark Ages, similarly, if a hermit lived alone he might inspire others, but probably his visitors left thinking only what a special person he was. Few would have been inspired to imitate him in his way of life. They'd have thought of him as if nodding at them from a cloud. Monastic communities, however, committed to lofty principles and radiating serenity and joy, projected a message that spread far and wide. Here were groups of individuals who had something everyone wanted, and whom everyone might be able somehow to emulate. Thousands flocked from far and near to join them in their way of life. Many others thought, "Perhaps

I, too, can be more charitable and peaceful in my own life."

The concept of cooperative communities offers the modern world a key to personal fulfillment which few can hope to discover on their own. By the example of such communities, and by the expansive consciousness they emanate, people everywhere can be inspired to seek a greater, inner fulfillment. No example can so convince others as one that is set by many people of many different temperaments, and from many different backgrounds, all of them dedicated to the same high ideal. That variety is, in fact, what cooperative communities attract naturally to themselves. It effectively contradicts any rationale offered that such people are special kinds of human beings, whose lives bear no relationship to their own realities.

If the hope for peace is realistic in this world, it must be sought first on a small scale, rather than through grand social reforms. Most important, always, is people's *individual* development. Without this focus, communities will have nothing they can offer others. Self-centeredness, even if one dwells in an earthly paradise, soon becomes suffocating to the adventurous spirit. Communities, in their example of all-embracing friendship, give a message of expansive self-identity.

It is therefore important that such communities seek also to objectify their inner development.

Every community should offer to the public some practical service in addition to whatever it does toward self-sustenance. Not to render such service to others would be to stagnate.

This service might take many forms. For instance, a community could develop a school for children. What sort of school? I wrote a book, called *Education for Life,* that proposes an enlightened system of education. This book has been praised by educators, and has been used for years in our own community schools under the name, "Living Wisdom" schools. Both the concepts and the curriculum were designed to promote a universal outlook on life and on truth. The teachings emphasize universal principles, rather than a specifically religious or sectarian teaching. If you prefer some other type of schooling, however, I suggest only that you promote also an outlook that is universal. High, *workable* ideals are greatly needed in today's world, where even children are inculcated with cynicism, and with a trivial outlook on life.

A community might also offer facilities for sharing with others whatever insights it has gained, and for sharing the ideals toward which it aspires.

The group might make a particular service of music and singing. Indeed, people are often more deeply affected by music that inspires than by well-worded discourses.

Communities might also send traveling groups out on tour as a means of sharing their principles—

emphasizing principles first, not the promotion of their own activities.

Still others might find inspiration in services that involve healing. Standard clinics might be established, provided the right personnel can be found. New healing methods might be explored also—for example, employing colors, sounds, and the creative application of energy.

Prayer for others can be a valuable service. I don't mean supplicating prayers, but healing energy sent out on waves of kindness and love while mentally holding in a force-field of light the persons one wants to help. Many experiments have been conducted along these lines, sufficient to convince even skeptics that *something* seems to be working with this practice. The persons for whom prayers were offered, in contrast to those in control groups who received no prayers, were reported as benefiting significantly.

Seminars could be offered to business corporations on enlightened business methods; to doctors, nurses, and hospital staffs on "cooperative healing," or on how to maintain a feeling of compassion for patients instead of hardening oneself in an effort not to absorb their unhappiness, oneself; to corporations of all kinds on the concept of enlightened leadership; to groups everywhere on how to succeed by focusing one's thoughts and energy, rather than by cutthroat competition; to individuals everywhere on methods of self-healing; to parents and teachers on the principles and techniques of enlightened child-raising; to single people on how to find a suitable mate; to couples passing through difficult times together on how to bring harmony and happiness to their marriage. The possibilities for meaningful sharing are unlimited. What is important is the *willingness* to let others know about any discoveries you've made. In upwardly progressive communities there are bound to be innumerable such discoveries.

Cooperative communities are not the same thing as *cooperatives*. The difference lies more in emphasis than in practice. A "cooperative," as contrasted to a cooperative community, is distinguished by the fact that every member has only one vote regardless of the amount of his investment. In cooperative communities, however, decision-making requires no such definition, for everyone automatically has the same status. Voting, therefore, is less likely to be an issue.

The practice of voting is in any case neither wholly fair nor so wholly democratic as people generally believe. Where large numbers of people are involved, or where it is important that an issue be voted on, the best way to decide matters may be by ballot. For small groups, however, voting poses several significant disadvantages.

Consider majority rule: It is certainly not always true that the majority knows best. One person in the group may even see a truth more clearly than anyone else. If an issue is voted on, that person may be outvoted. If, however, everyone knows that person from experience to be often right, a group that wants to be guided by truth, rather than by mere opinion, may realize that in this case voting may be the wrong way to settle the issue.

Another problem with voting is that having winners means also having losers. Why, in a genuine democracy, should anyone have to lose? Is not compromise possible? Cannot both sides be satisfied? Often, in small groups, they can be.

Finally, the system of deciding everything by vote forces everyone to be either for an issue or against it. Some of the members, however, may not feel convinced either way. Having to vote when uncertain may force them to unnatural conclusions. Once people have voted, moreover, they may consider their vote a commitment, to which they must remain loyal no matter how they come to feel about it later on.

On the other hand, I do not recommend rule by consensus. When consensus on every issue is required, it obliges the members to agree even if they don't feel competent to decide. In such circumstances, they will agree to a proposal simply to let the proceedings go on, and not because it has their heartfelt consent. Voting in such cases becomes merely routine. People cease, in time, even to interest themselves in the process.

Formal voting systems, designed to ensure cooperation, are often an effective way of *minimizing* cooperation. The fear is that, without them, a leader might bully others into doing his will. Maybe so, but in small groups the decisions are not often so vital that they endanger anything or anyone very much. If a leader shows this bullying weakness, he can be replaced if and when necessary. Or he may simply learn to behave better, in time. No human quality is indelible.

Obviously, at community meetings there must be free discussion, so that people may be given a chance to express themselves. Thus, reactions can be invited that might in the voting process become too formalized. Many issues can be decided, as I said, in favor of more than one side. Often, people don't have to be either for or against an idea. If some of them want one thing, and others, something else, can't both sides be satisfied? There are times, of course, when a yes or no decision is necessary; there are also times when a formal vote is needed. If the discussion leader in these circumstances omits to ask for a show of hands, there will always be people to remind him of this courtesy. No actual rule in the matter is necessary.

One may safely assume that most members of a cooperative community will want whatever is best for everyone; indeed, a *cooperative* community must be predicated on this assumption. If this spirit is lacking, the community will not succeed. There are plenty of communities—the average township, for example—where people think only of promoting their own interests. What I mean by *cooperative communities* is groups of people for whom living and working together harmoniously, with interest in the good of all, is a basic principle.

In times of nationwide economic collapse, a further benefit may be considered from such communities. They may form a network of cooperative communities across the country, each one specializing in manufacturing or producing certain items for which the others will be natural customers. In this case, the network may even establish its own internal currency. This was what one township in America actually did during the depression years of the 1930s.

At the same time, cooperative communities should not separate themselves in spirit from the greater society. In this respect, examples of communities like the Mennonites are anachronisms. We cannot set the calendar back three hundred years: Our present needs are too great.

In the members' attitude toward the world at large also—in their dress, their speech, their behavior—they would do well to blend as much as possible with the rest of society. They should not, of course, sacrifice their integrity or their ideals. For example, if a group decide to be vegetarian, they shouldn't compromise, but neither should they flaunt their eccentricity. Only by building bridges to society at large can cooperative communities become an influence for improving life everywhere. Thus, they can inspire thousands to embrace ideals at which, nowadays, it is fashionable to sneer—as if noble aspiration were merely "relative" and unworthy of honest consideration. The more inspiration you can share with others, the more inspiration you'll find, yourself.

What is always needed, in addition, is *upward* aspiration—aspiration of the heart, not of the head only. For aspiration without love is like an archer's bow without a string.

Cooperative communities are an eminently workable alternative for people everywhere who seek meaning in their lives. I say this from many years of personal experience, and from observation of the lives of numerous educated, intelligent, and *aware* individuals. With this ideal in mind there is indeed—I say it with conviction—hope for a better world!

ABOUT THE AUTHOR

J. Donald Walters was born in Romania of American parents. His father was an oil geologist for Esso (Exxon), and ultimately became Esso's chief geologist for Europe. In France, years later, he was awarded the Legion of Honor.

Mr. Walters received his early education in Romania, Switzerland, and England. Shortly after he'd turned thirteen, World War II began and his family moved to America for the duration. He received his higher education at Haverford College and at Brown University.

Internationally known as a lecturer and author, he speaks nine languages, of which he has lectured in five. Presently he lives near Assisi, Italy, lecturing in Italian (continuing, however, to write in English).

In the present book he focuses a lifetime of experience on the subject of communities and their potential importance in the evolution of modern thought. Advice he often gives to other writers of philosophy is, "Persuade people by sweet reason alone. Do not pound them over the head with your credentials, nor confuse them with ungrounded logic. Let conviction come to them by recognition, based on their own experience of life."

INDEX OF LITERARY WORKS

GENERAL INDEX

Important reading...be prepared to take on a new view of reality and your own nature. **Out of the Labyrinth** *is thought-provoking, intelligent, and filled with remarkable wisdom. This book belongs in any thinking/feeling person's library.*

—Fred Alan Wolf, Ph.D.
physicist and author of
Taking the Quantum Leap
and *The Spiritual Universe*

This book is wonderful. **Out of the Labyrinth** *is completely in harmony with the findings of modern science, yet it provides them with deep meaning. This message must spread everywhere.*

—Leon Kolb, Professor of Anthropology,
Emeritus, Stanford University

I found **Out of the Labyrinth** *a lucid complementary statement to the "either-or" assumptions of Western thought, as well as a much-needed affirmation of the limitations of trying to apprehend reality only through the mechanism of reason.*

—Rene Dubos, microbiologist,
Pulitzer Prize for *So Human an Animal*

An engaging and compelling argument for the continuing relevance of spirituality to modern life. From the Greek philosophers to quantum theory, Walters makes solid observations that lead us to question the dogmas of modern "truth." This is both a very good read and interesting journey into one of the finer minds of our time.

—Reverend Chip Wright,
Unitarian Universalist Church, Yakima, WA

A New Approach to the
Problem of Meaninglessness

The last hundred years of scientific and philosophical thought have created dramatic upheavals in how we view our universe, our spiritual beliefs, and ourselves. Commonly accepted theories of evolution and relativity, and the precepts of existentialism, have shaken the foundations of traditional religious practices. Many people now wonder if enduring spiritual and moral truths even exist.

Out of the Labyrinth presents fresh insight and understanding into this most difficult problem. In clear and accessible language, J. Donald Walters demonstrates the genuine compatibility of scientific and religious values and how, in fact, scientific discoveries and our most cherished moral values actually enrich and reinforce one another. Walters convincingly lays out a new approach to spirituality that solves the problem of meaninglessness and champions the possibility of human transcendence and divine truth. Hailed by both respected scientists and religious leaders alike, this book is a must read for anyone struggling to find answers to these daunting questions.

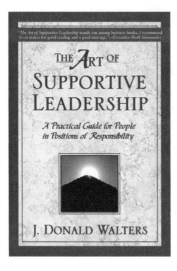

A great read the first time through and something to refer to again and again. The most depth and understanding of what a manager faces of the many management books I've read over the years. I plan to keep it on my desk as a daily reference.

—Ray Narragon, Sun Microsystems

The Art of Supportive Leadership *is brief, hits the points, and has a lot of common sense to it. We've been casting about for something like this for a long time. We use it in our Managers Training Workshop. This book is very practical, very readable, and concise.* **HIGHLY RECOMMENDED.**

—Kellog Corporation

A Proven Approach
to Successful Leadership

Do you want to improve your leadership skills and learn how to bring out the best in your employees, co-workers, or students? Then the *Art of Supportive Leadership* can help you! Large and small companies of every kind—from well-established industrial corporations to sparkling new tech firms—are using this proven approach to leadership with great success. It has become equally indispensable to the non-profit organizations, schools, and military personnel who also use it.

- ❀ Develop an inspiring vision
- ❀ Avoid ego games
- ❀ Build an effective team
- ❀ Win the loyalty of others
- ❀ Find creative solutions to difficult problems
- ❀ Combine intuition with common sense
- ❀ Run ahead of the pack
- ❀ Achieve lasting results

The Art of Supportive Leadership is defining the new cutting edge of leadership training. Drawn from the author's many years of successful leadership in numerous contexts, the book gives you clear and practical techniques that quickly produce results—even if you're new to leadership, and even if you can only devote limited time to improving your skills. Each chapter ends with short, concise summaries that serve as quick reference guides when you need them.

**For a free Crystal Clarity catalog,
or to place an order, please call:
800-424-1055, or 530-478-7600
Or visit our website at: www.crystalclarity.com**